CHANGE
THE WORLD,
CHANGE
YOUR LIFE

CHANGE THE WORLD, CHANGE YOUR LIFE

Discover Your Life Purpose Through Service

ANGELA PERKEY

Conari Press

First published in 2010 by
Red Wheel/Weiser, LLC
With offices at:
500 Third Street, Suite 230
San Francisco, CA 94107
www.redwheelweiser.com

ISBN: 978-1-57324-463-3
Library of Congress Cataloging-in-Publication Data is available upon request.

Cover and text design: Dutton & Sherman
Cover photograph, inset: © Tony Anderson/Digital Vision
Author photograph: © Bart Perkey
Production Editor: Michele Kimble
Copy Editor: Tania Seymour
Proofreader: Nancy Reinhardt

Printed in Canada
TCP
10 9 8 7 6 5 4 3 2 1

The paper used in this publication meets the minimum requirements of the American National Standard for Information Sciences—Permanence of Paper for Printed Library Materials Z39.48-1992 (R1997).

At least 10 percent of the author's proceeds will be donated through StudentsServe.org to Students Serve, the national nonprofit organization the author started to give money to college students so they can make a difference.

Contents

Part I
FINDING YOUR GLOBAL PURPOSE
13

v

Part II

CHANGING YOUR LIFE
65

Part III

CHANGING YOUR WORLD
121

A Q&A Session

Start by Reading This

Why is this important?

- There are 923 million people who do not have enough food to eat. This is equal to the number of people in the United States, European Union, and Canada.
- By 2030, there will be no more glaciers left in Glacier National Park.
- In the United States, 37.3 million people live in poverty. That's more than one out of every ten Americans.
- Nearly 7,500 people become infected with HIV *every day*.
- More than 47 million Americans do not have health insurance, making it nearly impossible to go to the doctor and get the medical care they need.

Although it's possible to go on and on with the statistics, this book isn't intended to be depressing. Instead, it's about enriching your life by doing what you can to make a meaningful difference in the world. You can use what you have—your skills, knowledge, and talents, to help change these statistics. In the process, you will also change your life. This book shows you how.

Can I really change the world?
Yes. You can improve the lives of others and solve local and global problems. To be sure, this is not "saving" the world, solving every problem that exists. No person is capable of doing this. However, you can start a nonprofit organization to provide service opportunities to college students (what I did) or join with friends to "adopt" an impoverished child in Africa or work to reduce your city's dependence on fossil fuels. There are infinite ways that you can make a meaningful impact. This book will inspire you with examples of people who have done this and will show you how you can as well. You do not have to be a millionaire, genius, or celebrity.

Will this change my life?
Without a doubt. By making a meaningful difference in this world, you will start to feel empowered. This isn't just about traditional community service. By combining your efforts to improve the world with your most ambitious goals and dreams, your life will gain meaning. You will realize that you have the ability to do great things and that you can change your life for the better. You'll build a living legacy and your actions will be remembered by others.

Do I have to be as wealthy as Bill Gates or Oprah?
No. This is about a new way of living, not just sending a huge check to charity. Many people think that simply writing a check will make a difference and absolve them from any social guilt or obligation to serve. They are wrong. As I explain later, nonprofit organizations are not doing enough to solve our problems. The government isn't off the hook either. Giving these institutions more money is not the solution. Despite the best efforts of the nonprofit industry and gov-

ernment programs, many of our global problems are getting worse. Because of this, it's up to everyday people to get involved.

Is it enough to just buy a Prius and eat organic vegetables?
Although driving a hybrid car and buying pesticide-free produce are steps in the right direction, you have much more to offer the community besides choosing to buy certain types of carrots at the grocery store! You have a mind and unique ideas and skills that can be used to solve local and global problems. This book shows you how you can make a much bigger difference, one that will be meaningful to you and your life. You owe it to yourself, your family, and your world.

Will this fit into my lifestyle?
Absolutely. I'll explain how you can work to solve the world problems you care about without adding an eighth day to the week. In the following pages, I've also interspersed motivating profiles of people, including an investment banker, working mother, med school student, and father of five, who have already done this. It's true that sometimes it is difficult to balance everything, but regardless of your professional, familial, or financial obligations, it is possible to make this work. I have broken down the process that has enabled me and many others to make a meaningful difference in the world.

Will this cost anything? Are my yearly donations enough?
Service doesn't have to cost anything at all. Even if you aren't in the habit of donating money to charities or church, a small amount can go a long way toward creating social solutions.

I've never volunteered before and have no interest in attending political rallies or joining interest groups. Is this okay?
Absolutely. Previous experience isn't necessary. Plus, changing the world and improving your life transcend partisan political bickering. This is about pragmatism, doing what you can; not activism.

My Journey

It was 2002, the summer after my freshman year of high school, and I was sitting in a nursing home painting the fingernails of yet another old lady. Her hands were shaking and lined with transparent blue veins. This must have been my fortieth hand that morning, and I had reached my limit. This was not my idea of service. My wonderful and well-intentioned mom had taken my younger sister and me to volunteer in a local nursing home every Monday, Wednesday, and Friday. She thought it would be good for us to spend some time volunteering over the summer, that this could help us become passionate about serving others. But it wasn't meant to be. Pushing old ladies in wheelchairs around a nursing home and painting their nails was simply not my thing, and I resented nearly all the time I spent there.

I knew there had to be a better way to give back to the community. I was young and inexperienced, but I was a hard worker with a solid mind. I thought these things had to count for something. Surely I had more to offer the world than my fingernail painting and bingo calling services!

I believed in volunteering and thought that what I was doing was helpful, but I was honestly not interested in making life better for people who could afford to live in private nursing homes. Because of this, I hardly cared about the outcome of what I was doing. I was more interested in making a difference in other ways—doing something about the high cost of nursing-home care or the rise of the uninsured population, for example. Now these were issues that I really cared about and that needed to be addressed. I became determined to make a meaningful difference in the world in a way that used my talents and interests.

My parents instilled in me the belief that giving money away to others and volunteering were integral parts of living well. I am infinitely grateful for their guidance and exemplary lifestyles, and I have worked to incorporate these practices into my own life now that I'm an adult. Yet serving others and giving donations to worthy causes didn't come naturally to me.

When I was in kindergarten, my dad took me to the bank, where I opened my first savings account. This was incredibly exciting. I now had a place to put my meager savings and all of the coins I had found. (I amassed a small fortune looking for dropped change wherever I went, earning me the nickname "Eagle Eyes.") Along with my new bank account, I began getting an allowance of fifty cents each week. I truly loved money, even at an early age.

There was a catch, though. My parents said that I had to give at least 10 percent of my allowance away as a tithe to church. If I wanted to give more as an offering, that was up to me, but the tithe was not optional. If I wanted to get an allowance, I had to start tithing.

Parting with a portion of my new cash inflow was not fun. Even though I had always seen my parents give away their money and they had explained why this was important, I didn't want to take part in tithing. I really liked going to church, but I didn't understand why I couldn't just keep all of the money. But in order to maintain my weekly income, I obliged and put the nickel in the offering plate each week. It wasn't easy, but I did it because I had to.

Eventually, it became less difficult for me to make charitable donations. It became a habit, and I started to realize that five cents was actually *not* that much money. I started to feel good about what the money would be used for, and I even gave more when I was feeling generous. As I grew older, I began to understand the importance of giving to others. The lessons have accumulated over time, and I have come to realize that all people have a need to live beyond themselves through service.

Each of us has been blessed with individual talents that we can share with others to improve the world. As I learned after volunteering at the nursing home, the key is to find a cause that matches your interests, skills, and life dreams. The result is a better world and a better life.

In college, I started a national nonprofit organization called Students Serve that gives college students money to make a difference in their communities. Serviceships fund innovative volunteer service projects. The idea is that students can use what they're learning in their courses to help solve the social challenges our world faces.

I decided to form the organization because I had become frustrated in my classes. We studied all kinds of global problems—

war, healthcare, global warming—but we weren't doing anything to *solve* them. I developed Students Serve so that college
students across the country could receive funding and use their
knowledge and creativity to improve their communities, nation,
and world in new ways.

By now, Students Serve has gotten fully off the ground and
has awarded multiple serviceships to college students. It's still
small in scale, but the grants fund quality student service projects that have the chance to really make a change in local and
national problems. In addition, I am engaging in service by running Students Serve on a volunteer basis. A team of students
from the College of William and Mary, my alma mater, oper-
ates everything, and we have a good time. We've even received
national press attention for our efforts. We are currently in the
process of expanding the organization through our newly re-
launched website, *www.StudentsServe.org*.

Most importantly, I can tell that I am making a difference in
the lives of others, and, in my own way, I'm changing the world.
The grants we are funding have made it possible for students to
help create a women's shelter, youth art program, community
garden, wheelchair recycling organization, and other effective,
original service programs.

My efforts to change the world through Students Serve have
truly changed my life as well. Working to start a nonprofit organization was a welcome diversion from my intense class work
at the College of William and Mary. Students Serve gave me a
creative and worthwhile way to connect with others and meet
new people. It also allowed me a time of intense inner reflection and soul searching when I was trying to form my own iden-

tity and decide "what I wanted to be when I grew up." Since that time, serving and giving to others has continued to enrich my life. Working in a corporate job, I have found that Students Serve and my volunteer work enable me to release stress, have fun, and do something important with my time that helps others. Watching the news, reading the paper, and studying world challenges are no longer as disheartening as they once were. I know that I am doing what I can to change these problems, and this gives me a sense of satisfaction and inner peace.

You Can Do It, Too

Before college, I would never have guessed that I would start a nonprofit organization. Yet sitting at a table covered in applications, surrounded by the volunteer team of students who ran Students Serve, I realized that each of us truly has the capacity to change the world.

You can do this, too. Some of us may make larger impacts than others, but this is not important. What's important is that we do what we can to improve the world we live in because doing so makes our lives meaningful and worth living. It fills us with the confidence to know that we can actively do something to solve our own problems and overcome the challenges our world faces.

In the coming sections, you will learn how to combine your strengths and personal ambitions so that you can be as effective as possible and create a meaningful change in the community. Then you will be able to determine how you can make an impact while still meeting your responsibilities and not disrupting your daily routines. I chose to start a nonprofit organization that is relatively small—at least for now. You certainly don't have to choose the same path. There are infinite ways for you to serve. Finally, you will learn how to keep making a meaningful difference, even after you've accomplished what you set out to do. You will build a legacy.

In these pages, you will find stories of people just like you who have done something with their lives that matters. These profiles are in no way intended to be boastful service resumes. Instead, these are inspiring examples of how all types of individuals can serve, regardless of whether they have created nonprofits that have raised hundreds of thousands of dollars or simply volunteered to teach people English whenever their busy schedules allowed. Each of these individuals have one thing in common— they have done what they could to improve the world. Their personal and insightful journeys will convince you that you have the ability to do something truly significant with your life, too.

There is no time to waste and no better time to get started. The problems of today will not be solved by complaining about the past or being pessimistic about the future. You have the power to do something. And you will.

At this point, I realize how far I've come since my days painting fingernails in the nursing home and mourning every cent given away to others. Giving to others has enriched my life and made it worth living. I assure you that by the time you finish this book, you will be amazed at everything you have done and at who you have become.

It's Your Turn.

PART I

FINDING YOUR GLOBAL PURPOSE

Before you jump in to change the world, it's essential to know the problems and issues that you're going to help solve. It can be overwhelming at the beginning. There are so many issues that need to be addressed! This section provides you with an accessible way to uncover the causes that are most important to you so that your efforts will be as successful and meaningful as possible.

Once you've discovered the target issue that you care about most, it's important to identify your ambitious life goals, talents, and passions. Although you may already know what you want out of life, it's always a good idea to periodically check in and make sure that you're on the right path. Goals and ambitions can change over time, and this part of the book will lead you through a simple and painless process that helps you unearth your most valued ambitions in every facet of your life—career, home/family, spirit, and community.

Once you identify your target cause, natural talents, and life goals, you have all the ingredients you need to change the world and your life. You simply have to fuse all of these pieces together to form your own, individual Global Purpose, which is your personalized way to make a meaningful difference.

CHAPTER 1

Diplomat 101

Beginning with the Basics

Service is the outer expression of your inner values.

When is the last time you did something that mattered, something that truly had a significant and lasting influence on your life or on the life of someone else? If you have trouble thinking of anything, that's okay. Many people are living lives that are unfulfilling. Many of us work over forty hours a week in jobs that are not personally satisfying and don't fully utilize our talents. Yet we want to live lives that matter and are worth remembering—lives that can make a meaningful difference, lives that can change the world. Seeing the endless stream of homeless people, sick children, and melting icecaps in the morning papers is sad and frightening. However, as I learned after starting Students Serve—and as you will see—anyone can make a meaningful difference in solving these problems and can live a satisfying and fulfilling life.

Reading this book will enable you to find your "world piece," your unique way to do your part to change the world. You'll also find an inner peace, a sense of contentment about your life. You will feel empowered by the knowledge that you have done something that really matters. You will also gain confidence and realize that you can accomplish your dreams.

Before getting started, it's important to lay a few things on the table.

1. Politicians, nonprofit organizations, and nongovernmental organizations (NGOs) have failed. This seems harsh, but for decades these institutions have made promises to solve our local and global challenges. Many have done good work and have helped millions of individuals, yet the problems that they were created to solve are still with us. A case in point is traditional food banks. They have fed billions of meals to people who would have otherwise gone hungry. This is an admirable and very important service, but the problem of world hunger still affects millions of people.

2. We're all in this together. To start making progress, we need individuals to come up with innovative ways to address our problems. This means that all types of people— from careful conservatives to diehard liberals, Southern belles to Northern Yankees, children to retirees, laboring immigrants to socialites—must contribute. This is democracy at its best.

3. Each of us can improve society. I have learned this through my own experiences and in interviews with others. Simply

stated, when we take it upon ourselves to do something to change the world, the results can be profound.

4. It doesn't take a village, at least not at first. Never before in the history of the world have individual people been as powerful as they are now. It only takes one person to ignite a movement that can improve communities.

Even if you've never volunteered or given money to charity, this is fine. No experience is necessary when it comes to changing the world.

SERVING FOR THE SOUL

Service, in its most basic form, is the outward manifestation of your inner beliefs. You are truly living out your values when you volunteer. Your beliefs are transformed from mere statements about global injustice, evil, or what is wrong in this world into productive actions that you can see, feel, and experience. It is the most sincere form of expressing what is in your soul. You are defining yourself and declaring what is important to you through your actions.

To make your efforts as meaningful as possible, I believe that it is important to connect your donations and volunteering to your inner satisfaction. When giving to others is personally important and has a positive effect on your life, you are more likely to continue making a significant difference. This is a newer and better way to give, serve, and change our world.

Give to Get

Giving to others provides a great sense of personal satisfaction, yet the idea that improving the world can have personal benefits is shocking to some people. "It is better to give than to receive" is a phrase we often hear. Many people believe that community service and monetary donations are purely altruistic, gifts to others or the world that provide no advantages to ourselves. However, if you think about it, volunteering and sending checks to charities do not leave the people who are giving empty-handed.

The clearest way to understand this is to focus on donations to nonprofit organizations. An overwhelming 92 percent of American households make financial contributions to churches, charities, and other groups. On the surface, this seems to be a selfless act, yet the organizations are not the sole beneficiaries of these generous donations. Individuals claim sizeable tax deductions for their donations.

Giving your time provides another type of benefit. Whenever people volunteer, they generally feel as though they have made positive contributions to society. This is gratifying and reinforces that these individuals are important to their communities. They feel good about themselves and their inner character. When they give to others, they receive internal self-worth. Giving is also about getting.

A Happier Life, A Happier World

Personal satisfaction with your life can lead to neighborhoods and societies that are better places to live. This is an important realization that is necessary to understanding how improving your life is closely associated with changing the world.

When you are unhappy, you probably do not treat others with kindness. For example, you are more likely to explode with anger when you get cut off by a rude driver (again!) or have to wait in line for twenty minutes at the bank. Because of your lack of personal fulfillment and patience, the bank tellers are likely to be agitated by your bad temper, and your frustrations lead to their irritability. When they go home following the end of their shifts, they are more likely to be cranky with their spouses and short-tempered with their children.

In this case, one person's unhappiness has affected an entire group of people. If we are living a hollow existence, we can cause other people to become unhappy as well. This is why it is crucial to live satisfying lives that fill us with contentment.

Scientific evidence has recently confirmed that happiness is contagious. Our internal well-being can affect the general well-being of our family members and friends, which can then be multiplied exponentially to all the people they know. Service, even seemingly small good deeds, leads to a more satisfying inner personal life. And when you feel positive about yourself, you share that internal joy with all the other people in your life. You change the world.

By serving others, you gain fulfillment and internal self-worth. The inner satisfaction you receive is passed on to the people around you, improving their lives and our communities.

TWENTY-FIRST-CENTURY SERVICE

Traditional community service and philanthropy do not empha-size the importance of personal connections to making a dif-ference. This is a problem, though, because we invest parts of ourselves every time we volunteer or donate money. My nursing home "fingernail episode" is the classic example of this. New and better ways to give money and serve are needed to have a more effective and meaningful impact on solving global problems.

A Better Way to Give

Most people give back to the community by donating their time, money, or both. But even if you have developed the admirable habit of making financial contributions to nonprofit organiza-tions, you oftentimes can't say with certainty that the donations were personally meaningful. The better way to give, as described later, will help you maximize both the effectiveness of your con-tributions and their personal significance to your life.

A Better Way to Serve

If you do volunteer work, increase the effectiveness of your ef-forts by volunteering at the same place whenever you're able, instead of going to a new organization each time. By doing this, you can form personal connections and relationships, and the organizations do not need to train you each time you are able to volunteer. You will already know the ropes and can even help new volunteers.

Using your particular talents and gifts can help you make an even bigger impact on solving a global problem. Someone who is trained as an accountant is likely going to engage in more effective and meaningful service if auditing a food bank's financial statements rather than stacking the cans. This definitely doesn't mean the accountant can't do both things, but using special skills and interests will make a much larger impact on the life of the accountant and the world problem.

"No act of kindness, no matter how small, is ever wasted."
—AESOP

■

Catalina Saldivar
"There was never a hesitation. This was what I needed to do. I needed to help in any way I could. It was basic, but it was a starting point for something great."

Working at a Marriott hotel, many of Catalina Saldivar's coworkers spoke Spanish and only a few phrases in English. Not being able to communicate made it incredibly difficult for them to function in America. They were frequently unable to read road signs, nutrition fact labels, government forms, and their kids' field trip permission forms. Without a working knowledge of English, they couldn't get driver's licenses, attend school, or help their children with homework problems. Above all, they wanted to be able to communicate with the people around them.

As Catalina got to know her colleagues, most of whom were housekeepers, they expressed their deep desire to learn English. Even though she had never been a teacher and had just received her associate's degree, Catalina decided to do something to help. She was bilingual and had taught Sunday School in the past, so she convinced herself that she had something to offer and could help her hardworking colleagues learn English. She used her own money to buy school supplies and developed a four-month curriculum. Classes were held every week at 7:30 in the morning.

Her efforts worked. By the end of Catalina's curriculum, her students had acquired a functional knowledge of English. Following completion of the course, they had a graduation ceremony in which the students dressed up in caps and gowns and had a chance to walk across a stage. This might have been the only opportunity the students would ever have to "graduate." During the ceremony, each of the graduates delivered a thank-you speech—in English. To Catalina, seeing the students interact with guests, using the English they had learned in her classes, was very rewarding. The program was so successful that the local school system adopted it so that an even greater number individuals who didn't speak English could learn the language.

"It's about taking care of others. It's about serving others. It's about the people. And this can be very rewarding."

■

This type of service is about putting your money where your heart is and your mind where your hands are. You invest yourself in solving a specific social problem. You combine your financial donations, mental talents, and your time to truly change the world.

To help clarify the difference, here's a comparison of the old and new ways to serve.

Old Way

Volunteer a couple of hours each month at a different place each time. You might not be really interested in what you're doing, but you feel like you have a duty to give back by donating your time.

New Way

Instead of volunteering as before, you ask for donations from local businesses and friends so that you can go on a one-week mission trip with your church. Together, you provide healthcare to people who cannot afford to go to the doctor in Guatemala. As your clinic leaves the village after a long day of seeing patients, a ten-year-old girl runs up and embraces you. Her huge smile is beaming at you with thanks. You know that you will never forget this experience.

Old Way

Your father, who loved historic architecture, recently passed away, and you and your siblings want to do something to honor his life and make his legacy live on. You, your brothers, and your sister each donate to a variety of charitable organizations that preserve historic buildings.

New Way

You and your siblings form a family foundation in your father's name. Your sister finds a building near his childhood home that is deteriorating and that he would have wanted to protect. You combine your money to buy it and restore the building to its original condition. You each spend a couple of weekends helping to paint the interior. The end result is terrific, and you donate the building to the city in hopes that it can be used to revitalize that area of town. Your dad would have been so proud.

- You don't have to be a philanthropist who buys a ticket to a $1,000-a-plate charity dinner. It's perfectly okay if you are not wealthy.
- You don't have to hold a diploma from an elite college. It's great if you do, but you can still solve world problems and make a meaningful difference if you have limited education.
- You don't have to be famous or influential in your community. Celebrities often use their star status to serve others and make a news splash, but this certainly isn't a prerequisite to making a difference.
- You don't have to have a lot of time on your hands. Your contribution can be meaningful to both yourself and the world, even if your project is short in duration.

You simply have to want to make a meaningful difference in your life and in the lives of others. The rest of this book is your guide to making this happen. If you're not already sure which world problem you want to tackle, the first part helps you choose a cause that you can be passionate about.

CHAPTER 2

133 Million Orphans

Discovering Your Cause

"Everybody can be great . . . because anybody can serve.
You don't have to have a college degree to serve.
You don't have to make your subject and verb agree
to serve. You only need a heart full of grace.
A soul generated by love."
—MARTIN LUTHER KING JR.

BEGINNING THE JOURNEY

From the 133 million orphans in the world to the deforestation of South America, choosing one cause or issue to focus on can be incredibly difficult. If you are like me and most other people, there are at least fifty different needs or issues that really energize you. You probably want to fix every single thing wrong with the world—and do it all at the same time.

Think of all the problems our world faces. Every time you turn on the TV, read the newspaper, or go online, you are confronted with all that is wrong around the globe. What you don't see is that normal, everyday people with jobs, families, hobbies, and other commitments are able to solve them.

Find Your Cause

Before I formed a nonprofit organization, I had to know what the organization would be working for. When I was first starting out, the issues I cared about most were student service grants, government debt, mental healthcare, high obesity rates, access to health insurance, and the exorbitant costs of higher education. I cared about the world, its people, and its many problems, yet it was next to impossible to try to do something about all of these things at the same time. I wasn't focused, and it became difficult for me to make a significant impact on each of these problems. I also realized that I wasn't as passionate about some of these issues as I originally thought I was. And that was okay. It's important to remember that the more you care about an issue or solving a problem, the more meaningful it will be when your efforts are effective. In the end, I chose to focus on providing student service grants and making the commitment to this one cause has made all the difference in terms of the effectiveness of the nonprofit.

Pick a Problem

You might already know what you're passionate about. Perhaps you've wanted to save the sea otter since you were seven years old and saw it at the zoo. That's great! However, if you're unsure what your cause should be, here are some ways to help you decide.

What Is Most Wrong with the World?

Take out a notebook and list everything you can come up with.

This is a significant undertaking and it may take a while to form a complete listing. When it comes down to thinking of all the world's problems, this can be somewhat overwhelming. There are so many, but the best way to start a list is with a five- to ten-minute marathon session during which you search your mind and soul for everything you want to change.

Please be sure not to sell yourself short and let self-doubt sink in, especially at this point. Don't question your ability to find a cure for cancer and refuse to add that to your list. Your goal right now is simply to write down everything that matters to you. From the inability of medical researchers to find a cure for malaria to the destruction of the redwoods in California to the lack of a playground at the local elementary school, your issues can be local, national, or global in scale.

Once you've finished, pull out this morning's newspaper or go online and read the headlines. What stands out to you? It's inevitable that you will find hundreds of different community and world problems. What stories do you want to read? What concerns you most? If you're like me, you may avoid reading certain articles because they cause you to become irritated and frustrated. What are these stories about? Although thinking about all the challenges our world faces seems pessimistic and negative, the good news is that you are going to help solve one of these problems.

Another way to tease out what really concerns you is to think about your conversations with other people. What gets you really excited or passionate? What are the issues and opinions that you refuse to compromise when debating or discussing world affairs with someone else?

Crystal Globe

When I was in elementary school, my two best friends and I would have sleepovers and play Dream, a game we invented and were very proud of. Basically, we imagined what our lives would be like when we were older. We created fabulous dreamlike scenarios about going on extravagant cruises and meeting the nicest millionaire bachelors in the world who also happened to have great bodies and brilliant smiles. We decided that we would all become doctors, marry the millionaires, have kids, be next-door neighbors, and create perfect lives for ourselves.

Take a moment now to indulge yourself, just for a few minutes, with Crystal Globe, an updated version of Dream. The object of this is to come up with something that seems impossible now but would make the world a better place in the future. Here are some examples I've come up with:

- Someday, there will be no garbage cans or trash collectors. Humans will produce so little trash that these things will simply be unnecessary.
- Eventually, the word "orphan" will no longer appear in the dictionary. Every child will have a home.
- There will be a time when every person will know how to read. Adult illiteracy programs will only exist in history books.

- In fifty years, cancer will be eradicated, just as polio was in the last century.

If you uncover any additional issues you are care about while going through this exercise, you can add these to your list as well. Thinking of the impossible is not a waste of your time. Despite hearing lectures about the impossibility of keeping humans from contracting viruses, Jonas Salk believed he could find a way to immunize people. In the 1950s, he developed the polio vaccine. His efforts have saved the lives of countless people.

When I Was Your Age, Pluto Was a Planet

Here's another way to think of how you can create an ideal global community and uncover what your cause should be. Seniors can often be heard saying something such as, "When I was your age, we didn't have toilets. No one did. We all used outhouses." When I was in first grade, we were told that Pluto was a planet. However, scientists have recently backtracked and said that Pluto is too small to be a planet.

If you could have a conversation with your great, great, great grandchildren after you die, what would you want to tell them about how the world they inhabit is different from the world you lived in?

Here are some ideas to help you get started:

- When I was your age, we had an endangered species list of animals we thought were going to disappear from the Earth forever.

- When I was your age, there were thousands of different languages spoken across the globe. This led to miscommunication between political leaders and almost caused global warfare.
- When I was a child, there wasn't a medication that cured heart disease, so most people died before they reached one hundred years old.

Hopefully, these are getting you to think about how you want to improve the world.

SPHERE OF SERVICE

Most of us are inclined to want to solve everything at once. However, by focusing your service, you will make a more meaningful difference and actually be able to see the results. For a girl who grew up collecting canned foods, visiting sick people, cooking for the homeless, and doing almost every type of community service possible, this was atypical for me. But it made all the difference in how effective my efforts with Students Serve were.

Now that you've made a list of issues you care about, it is important to narrow it down to one or two specific focus areas. That's it—only one (maybe two). Finding a cure for cancer is ambitious enough. Trying to find a cure for cancer while working to end child labor abuse around the globe will probably be overwhelming! Choosing a specific issue to target may be difficult at first, but it is important. Once you do this, we'll call it your *Sphere of Service,* the issue on which you will concentrate the majority of your efforts.

Don't be ashamed to take issues off your list. It certainly doesn't mean that you are heartless. It just means that you will be concentrating on solving a problem that is more personally significant. Your work will be more meaningful and you'll probably be able to make a larger impact. There is no shame in not caring about every single injustice or problem in the world. We are most zealous about the issues that affect us personally, and this is not a bad thing at all.

Where Are the Greatest Needs?

While you are narrowing down your list, you might want to think about which problems are being overlooked. There are a lot of organizations that focus on world peace, but how many people out there care about providing books to poor children? How could you make the biggest impact?

Take some time to really go through your list and reflect. Brew some hot herbal tea, relax in the hammock, or curl up on your favorite sofa so that you can get comfortable and think deeply.

GAINING UNDERSTANDING

Congratulations! Now that you have your Sphere of Service, it's time to do some fact finding so that you can really understand your issue and know the best way to make a meaningful difference.

You don't have to be a professional researcher or have a PhD to do this. Even if you dread the idea of going to the library or opening up a book, that's fine; there are many different ways to do your research and and there are several reasons why it is so important.

1. Understand the issue and make sure it interests you. By doing a little research, you will either confirm that you want to do something about the Sphere of Service you have chosen, or you will realize that it's not for you. If the latter is the case, you can just go back to your list of problems and try again. It's no big deal.

2. Find out what the true causes of the problem are. Your goal is to find out why the problem you've chosen exists. Why do the homeless people in San Francisco spend the day lying in the park instead of getting a job? Why do children in Mobile, Alabama, score poorly on standardized tests? You will find the root causes of the problem. Oftentimes, only the symptoms are visible. A woman might not be willing to leave her abusive husband. That's the problem, but why doesn't she leave? She can't find a job to support herself and her three kids. There's the root cause.

3. Learn what needs to be done. By looking at what other organizations are doing to solve the problem, you will see that there is much more work to do. Even though there are national organizations raising money to provide medications to AIDS patients, millions are still dying every year. Even

with the local food bank, there are people who are going hungry. Needs are not being met. If they were, the problem would no longer exist.

4. Establish credibility. It was crucial for me to prove to potential donors and supporters that I really understood the need for student service grants, my Sphere of Service. By sharing the research I had done about the lack of grants, people realized that providing grants to college students was really important to me and to our country. I was not simply trying to add a few lines to a resume—I was serious. I didn't have to write newspaper articles about my issue or do anything extraordinary. I just had to be able to explain that I knew all about the problem I wanted to solve.

5. Think of ideas about how to structure a solution. You will be able to discover new, better ways of doing something to solve the global problem that concerns you most.

Let's get started.

Fact Finding

Go online and search for your issue. If you are doing something that many people are concerned about, such as helping homeless people, you will likely find numerous organizations that are also trying to solve the problem. This is a good thing, and it means that you probably won't have a difficult time finding the information you need.

Simply go through their sites looking for any facts, statistics, graphs, and other pieces of information. Print out what you think is most interesting and compelling. If you see any shocking facts or statistics that make you energized about finding a solution, these are the things you want to become familiar with.

However, if your issue is more obscure, you may have difficulty finding information online. For example, you might be trying to find a cure for a rare disease that your friend has just been diagnosed with. When searching the issue, you may not come up with helpful information. It may be that there's nothing out there. The best thing to do in this case is to go to your local library. Don't worry if you've never been there or if you always walk by the reference section. The librarians will show you the way. In all likelihood, they will help you find plenty of information.

FIVE WHYS

First, be sure to look into why your problem exists. Oftentimes, the real cause of a problem is not something obvious. For example, the news usually reports only the horrible after-effects. The way to determine the root cause of your issue is to use the "Five Whys" method. Here's how:

Ask why your problem is occurring; then ask why the problem still exists. Then do it again until you've "asked why" five times or have come to the true cause of the problem.

The best way to understand how the Five Whys method works is to look at an example.

Sphere of Service: **International child hunger and malnutrition**

Why are children starving around the world?

They do not have enough nutritious food to eat.

Why do they not have enough nutritious food to eat?

Their parents are poor and they do not have enough money to buy healthy foods for their children.

Why are their parents poor?

They have jobs that pay menial wages.

Why do they keep jobs that only pay menial wages?

They can't get better jobs.

Why can't they get better jobs?

They don't have the education or skills that are necessary to get jobs that pay higher wages.

We've found one of the root causes of child hunger. So why are there children starving around the world? One reason is that their parents have low-paying jobs that don't provide enough income to purchase nutritious foods. It's important to note that this is an oversimplification of the issue of child hunger. Most of the time, there are numerous root causes of a problem. However, this is a good thing because it's impossible to solve every root cause at one time. You are going to start off by solving one of these problems. If you want, you can move on to other causes later. But for now, we are just looking for one specific root cause.

The Five Whys method should help you find the underlying cause or causes that keep your problem from being solved. It's simply a thought exercise, but once you understand what *is* being done and what *isn't* and, you will see where you can step in to help.

If you don't know the answers to your "why" questions, you might need to do additional fact-finding. If the problem is well-known, there is likely a wealth of information on the Internet. Be mindful that some organizations may only try to find temporary answers to the symptoms of the more important underlying problems and may avoid discussing the root causes on their websites. Your goal, however, is to stop the problem from occurring in the first place, so it's important to dig deeper to find the information you need.

The Need

Now that you have pinpointed at least one root cause of your Sphere of Service, you need to know what is already being done to address the problem. Look at other nonprofit and government websites to see if they are doing anything. Be sure to go through several organizations because their efforts frequently overlap. To help you figure out where the greatest needs are, you need to answer the following questions:

- Are there any geographic areas that are being overlooked?
- Is this problem being addressed in all places that are afflicted by it?

- What needs are not being filled?
- Are the nonprofits and local governments already doing a good job? If yes, what additional resources do they need?
- Are all of the people who are affected by this problem being helped?
- Are people or organizations in other cities, states, or nations solving this problem in a way that can be adapted to your location?

GETTING INTO THE WORLD

Finally, now that you thoroughly understand your Sphere of Service, it's time to get offline and dive into the real world. If your problem affects local people, go talk to them. Make sure you really understand why and how they have been affected. Question how you can prevent this from happening, and get the view from their perspectives. I must issue a note of caution here. Some people may be offended by your efforts to help. Try to be sensitive and understand their stories, and make sure to tell them your intentions.

Visit local nonprofits, foster-care homes, soup kitchens, or church ministries. See what they are doing and offer to volunteer for a couple of hours. Going online or looking up "homeless shelter," "humane association," or another type of nonprofit in the White/Yellow Pages should provide you with plenty of options. In addition, you can probably find organizations that need volunteers by looking in the newspaper. Many papers have a community section that lets nonprofits post their immediate service needs. You can even check the Volunteers section of Craigslist for postings made by local organizations and groups of citizens. Below are some websites that can lead you to volunteer opportunities. You might want to visit several of these because many of the opportunities are only listed on one site.

- Volunteer Match
  www.volunteermatch.org
- Volunteers of America
  www.voa.org
- Points of Light
  www.pointsoflight.org
- 1-800-Volunteer
  www.1-800-volunteer.org
- Idealist
  www.idealist.org

While you are volunteering, make note of how things could be done more effectively, and think about the needs that are still not being met. Talk to the other volunteers, and see what they have learned and why they are there. Then, think about how you can work together with the nonprofit to make an even larger impact. You might even want to speak with a staff member about this. They will most likely be glad to have your help.

In addition, you can talk to others in the community. Are your friends, people at your church, and city leaders concerned about this problem? What do they think can be done to make a change?

Use everyone that you talk with as a sounding board. Tell them your ideas and listen to their thoughts. See what they think and pay attention to their suggestions. I can't tell you how invaluable other people's advice was to me when I was first starting Students Serve. Some of the people I talked to helped me avoid major problems later on.

By now, you are the resident expert on your focus issue. Congratulations! Now it's time to uncover your personal ambitions for a better life so that you can combine them with your Sphere of Service.

CHAPTER 3

Mirror, Mirror on the Wall . . .

Uncovering What Matters to You in Life

"I don't know what your destiny will be, but one thing I know: The ones among you who will be really happy are those who have sought and found how to serve."
—ALBERT SCHWEITZER

Now that you've identified your Sphere of Service, it's important to examine your personal strengths and goals. By uncovering your life dreams and ambitions, you will be able to combine these with your Sphere of Service. While solving your portion of the world's problems, you will also be creating the type of life you desire.

■

David Fajgenbaum

"Being able to honor Mom meant so much. I could do
something proactive despite the hard times."

On July 17, 2003, David Fajgenbaum's mother, Anne Marie Fajgenbaum, was diagnosed with terminal brain cancer. At the time, he
was a freshman in college, and this news was emotionally devastat-
ing. Coping with his mother's illness while adjusting to the rigors
of college life was a challenge, and David found that there were
no adequate resources on campus to help him deal with this very
personal and difficult situation. Knowing that his mother did not
have long to live, he began coming home every weekend to spend
whatever time he had left with his family.

David's mom was deeply concerned about how he would handle her death and move forward with his life. David wanted to do
anything he could to reassure her that everything would be all right
and that he and his sisters would be fine. Shortly before his mother
passed away, David promised her that he would form a support
network in her honor for students like himself who were coping
with the loss of a friend or family member. He wanted to make
sure that they were not suffering in silence. Using her initials for
the name of the organization, he started Students of AMF (Ailing
Mothers and Fathers) on campus.

David's friends were very encouraging and wanted to get involved. This quickly led to the expansion of the campus chapter
into a national organization, now called National Students of
AMF. Since 2006, more than eighty universities have contacted
AMF about starting a chapter. The organization has also been featured on the *Today Show* and in *Reader's Digest*.

David has more than fulfilled the promise he made to his mother. He recently graduated from Oxford with a master's degree in public health and is currently studying to become a surgical oncologist. He had always known that he wanted to become a doctor, but his mother's diagnosis and subsequent death helped him focus his attention. Now, he wants to be able to help people like his mom.

Starting National Students of AMF helped David channel his grief and emotions into something positive. In the moments when he was overcome with sadness and feelings of helplessness, he channeled his energy into developing the organization, sometimes working all night. It also gave him a way to connect with his father and sisters despite their grief. The family was able to unite around a good cause and help other people dealing with the loss of a loved one. They were able to remember their mother and honor her memory while continuing to live their lives.

UNCOVERING YOUR STRENGTHS

By using your strengths and natural talents to make a difference in your Sphere of Service, your efforts will be as effective as possible. As a trained pianist, you could teach low-income children to play the piano. Instead of cleaning the animal cages at a shelter, you could use your IT skills to design a website that features each of the animals and allows people to adopt online.

You probably already have a general idea of your natural talents and strengths. However, I have found that it's helpful to remind yourself of your true gifts so that you can continue to use them as well as possible. Below are some basic questions to get you started on this process. It's a good idea to write your responses down. When you're finished, you can go back through your answers and see if any themes or patterns emerge.

What Are You Good At and What Do You Enjoy?

- What do you consider to be your biggest accomplishment?
- What can you do better than anyone else?
- Which skills do you use in your job?
- How do you like to spend your time outside of work?
- Do you have any hobbies?
- Are you a people person or do you prefer behind the scenes work?
- What do people give you compliments on?
- What characteristics make you stand out from your friends and siblings?

What Are Your Weaknesses?

- Is there anything you detest doing?
- What's the most embarrassing thing you've ever done?
- Is there anything you would refuse to do, even for $100,000 a year?
- Which classes did you dislike in school?

Now that you have a basic awareness of your likes, dislikes, and what you're really good at doing, let's take a quick check and determine what your personal ambitions are. After you do this, you will be able to combine your Sphere of Service, strengths, and life dreams in order to determine the most meaningful and effective way for you to serve the world.

Wishing Well

Examining your personal ambitions may seem unusual in the context of giving to others. However, the importance of doing so cannot be underestimated. Service can change your personal life—how you think, who you interact with, how you spend some of your time and money—in addition to the outside world. It is critical that your service efforts help you accomplish your dreams in life. When you are achieving your goals, you feel good about yourself and are likely to reflect that inner fulfillment on others.

For these reasons, the importance of personal motivation and the effect that your efforts will have on your life, it is imperative that you outline your ambitions. After this is finished, you will be able to combine your Sphere of Service, strengths, and ambitions to form a customized way for you to solve global problems.

YOUR FOUR LIFE GOALS

Break your life goals down into the areas that are most important to you—your career, home and family, spirit, and community.

For some people, pinpointing their ambitions for life is not difficult. They are on a clear-cut career path, and they know exactly what they want. They know that in two years, they want to make partner or be promoted to assistant manager or get married. For others, defining a set of life goals and ambitions may not be so easy. They may be at a defining point in their lives and need to make an important decision, such as whether or not to attend graduate school, have children, or quit a dead-end job to start a business.

Working through the four keystone areas of your life can help you determine what you truly want to accomplish in the next few years. As you did for discovering your strengths and interests, I think it's helpful to write down your ideas. You will probably want to add to your list at some point in the next couple of days as your mind has time to really digest and think through this again.

For me, defining my life ambitions was somewhat challenging. As I continued to think about this, my mind kept coming up with new things I wanted to do with my life. I would wake up before my alarm with excitement, realizing that I suddenly had a burning desire to go to Argentina and talk with native Spanish speakers or take an art class on mosaic pottery.

Who knows what you will come up with? Be sure not to confine yourself at this point because you can work around personal obstacles. For now, just let go. Release any reservations or hesitations that you may have.

Really think about what you want. What would change your life? When you are sitting in a nursing home telling your new neighbors who you are and what you did with your life, what do you want to be able to tell them?

Career

You spend the majority of your waking hours at your job. Life is too short to only live for the weekends, which represent less than a third of every year. If you're still a student, this applies to you, too.

- How do you want to spend the majority of your time during the day?
- Is your current job interesting to you?
- Do you want to stay with this employer?
- Do you like the people you are working with? Are they encouraging, friendly, and generally pleasant to be around?
- If you could get any job in the next six months, what would it be?
- If you could get any job in the next few years, what would it be?
- What is your least favorite part of your current job?
- What do you love doing in your current position?
- What career change would really excite you?
- What do you want to accomplish professionally before you are no longer working?

Home and Family

Here, consider your desires for your personal and family life and their interactions with your work. This includes your family, personal finances, hobbies, and other interests.

- How do you want your family to change over the next three years?
- Do you want to get married, have a baby, repair a relationship, reconnect with relatives you haven't seen since childhood?
- Are you spending too much time at work?
- What will your family need over the next few years?
- Is your income sufficient for maintaining the type of lifestyle you and your family want?
- Could you survive with a lower income?
- How important is it to both you and your family that you make more money?
- How can you be a better mother, father, sister, brother, niece, granddaughter, stepdaughter . . . ?
- What's the status of your relationships with your parents, brothers, sisters, grandparents, and other relatives?
- Do you want to move so that you can be closer to family?
- Does your home need improvement?
- Do you want to go on an extended vacation?
- Where do you want to travel?
- What personal financial obligations do you need to take care of now?

- Will there be any additional financial changes that will arise in the next two years?
- How will these affect your life, not just your finances?
- What hobbies do you have that you want to maintain?
- What additional activities have you always wanted to do but just never gotten around to doing?
- How will you fit these into your life?

Spirit

Next, you're going to delve into your spiritual and religious beliefs to find out if anything is missing and how you want to grow. Please do not skip over this section because it seems difficult! Avoiding these questions over time ultimately leads to an unfulfilling life. Don't do this to yourself. Your life is too important to waste by avoiding difficult questions.

- Is your daily life a reflection of your religious beliefs? If not, how do you want to change this?
- Have you thought about what will happen to you when you die?
- What do you need to learn about your religious beliefs?
- Do you want to start going to church or find another place of worship?

- Have you brushed aside any religious/spiritual questions recently because they seem too difficult to answer?
- Have your values changed?
- What would make your religious beliefs more meaningful to you?
- Do you need to spend more time in quiet, reflective thought?
- Have you read anything recently that challenged your beliefs?

Community

Finally, it's important to analyze what you want from your non-family relationships and community in the next couple of years.

- Do you want to meet new friends who have different lifestyles?
- Would you like to become a better friend to others?
- Do you want to strengthen the bonds that you have with your current friends?
- Do you want to be more involved in community affairs; that is, local politics, your church, local nonprofit organizations, civic groups, your child's school, etc.?
- What parts of town do you want to explore that you've just never gotten around to?
- Do you want to stay in this community or do you want to move somewhere else?

- What types of local people do you want to meet?
- Are there any events you want to attend, support, or get involved in?

Anything Missing?

Although there are a variety of different questions listed above, check to be sure that something isn't missing. Do you have any other goals for your life, things you want to do, places you want to see, skills you want to gain, milestones you want to reach? Go back over your list of ambitions and double check that you've got everything. If you think of anything else, now's the time to go ahead and write it in.

CHAPTER 4

Your Global Purpose

Uniting Your Cause with Your Goals

"The person born with a talent they are meant to use
will find their greatest happiness in using it."
—JOHANN WOLFGANG VON GOETHE

At this point, you know your strengths, ambitions, and Sphere of Service. Now all you have to do is decide on a specific way to combine everything and create an effective way for you to solve the problems you care about. This is where the process really starts to get exciting. You are going to change your world and your life.

In the past few years, there have been a lot of books published about finding your true purpose in life. However, I believe many people get trapped trying to decipher exactly why they were created and what they should do with their lives. Dwelling on the details of their life, many individuals become frustrated when they feel like they don't know what their one "true purpose" is. Yet I believe that the question should not be about finding our purpose. We were all created for the same purpose, to serve and love the Creator, ourselves, each other, and the Earth. Instead, the question should be *how* each of us can fulfill this purpose to the best of our abilities. This is an important distinction. Developing a Global Purpose for your life defines how you plan to integrate your goals, natural talents, and service in a way that reflects your values.

■

Becca Stevens
"Service has created a
beautiful community for my family."

Becca Stevens is not your typical priest. In addition to her duties as chaplain of St. Augustine's Chapel at Vanderbilt University, she has developed Magdalene, an organization that provides housing and a nurturing community to women who are trying to regain their lives and sense of self following prostitution.

Many of the women who live at Magdalene previously had been trapped in a seemingly endless cycle fueled by drug abuse. In order to finance their addictions, many of them had taken to the streets of Nashville to sell their bodies. To these women, Magdalene represents a chance to start a new life, one free from the grasp of drugs, prison, and physical abuse. While living in the Magdalene home free of charge, they have the opportunity to undergo 12-step treatment programs, physically recover, and share their experiences with women and counselors who understand. They can be loved.

Believing in the importance of showing love through service, Becca started Magdalene in 1996. She was sexually abused at a church function when she was seven years old, and in some ways, starting Magdalene has enabled her to heal. Although she didn't make the connection before starting the home for former prostitutes, she has come to the realization that everything bad that happens in life can be used for good.

Magdalene continues to grow, and the organization has even developed its own line of lotions and body-care products called Thistle Farms. The high-quality products are made by the residents and are sold to benefit the organization. This is a fun and profitable way for the women to express their gratitude for the opportunity to live at Magdalene.

> "There are a lot of problems in this world,
> but we can do something to help."

■

YOUR GLOBAL PURPOSE

Your Action
To form your personal Global Purpose, first look at your Sphere of Service. Now, define exactly what you can do to address this problem.

Here are some examples of actions you can take:

- Provide GED study guides to women living in abusive households in Kansas City so they can find independence through employment.
- Lower the cost of contraceptives so that low-income women in Uganda can afford them, which will help to prevent the spread of HIV/AIDS.
- Offer educational after-school activities to children in Athens, Georgia, who would otherwise be without adult supervision after the school day ends.

Your Passion

Next, go back and review your ambitions. How can you tie any of these into the actions that can solve your Sphere of Service problem?

If your vision for a better world is to increase children's access to books in your local community and your ambition is to get promoted at work, you could start a book drive at your company and several other businesses around town. The books you collect could then be donated to low-income kids in public schools.

You would be accomplishing several things at the same time here. First, you would be addressing a problem that you deeply care about, changing the world in your own way. Plus, you would have proved to your boss that you can take charge. You can lead other people and take the initiative. An added benefit is that since you've been collecting books in your company, employee morale has likely improved. It's a better place to work. Your chances of getting a promotion are much higher.

There's another benefit. While collecting books from other businesses, you've made networking connections that will be useful even if your supervisor doesn't put you in a position of greater responsibility. You can use those connections to get another job.

Socially, you've probably talked with several people who are completely different from yourself. They are all ages and have different jobs, incomes, and interest areas. You have really enjoyed connecting with them and have even made some new friends. You have changed your life.

Before starting Students Serve, I realized that I wanted to meet new people and gain leadership experience. The best way for me to do this was to start a nonprofit organization run by college students to provide academic service grants to other college students.

There are many ways that serving others can enhance your life as well as theirs. Here is a small selection of ways service can improve the many facets of people's lives.

Work Life

- Gain management experience
- Explore new career opportunities
- Represent employers in the community
- Connect with colleagues outside the office
- Network
- Get business ideas

Personal Life
- Meet a future spouse
- Reduce stress
- Make new friends
- Discover a hobby
- Have good, cheap fun

Finally, consider what your strengths are and how you can use your natural talents to contribute. Go back to what you wrote down. What is the best way for you to make your vision happen? How can you contribute as much as possible?

For instance, if you are a born public speaker, you should probably be out in the forefront, educating people about the issue you're going to solve. If your vision is to equalize salaries for women and men in your hometown, it's important for employers to know that this problem actually exists. In your research, you learn that many employers discount women's pay for lack of time spent on the job. Many have had to take career breaks in order to raise children. To correct this inequality, you might want to contact local groups of business executives and tell them of your concern. They may agree to let you speak for five minutes at their next meeting.

If public speaking isn't your thing, you can still solve the same problem but without getting up in front of crowds. If your strength is being really detail oriented, you might begin a letter-writing campaign to inform business executives of the problem of unequal pay. You advise them to analyze the salaries that they pay men and women in similar positions and consider the career paths and personal lives of their employees. You urge them to correct any inconsistencies.

There are endless examples of how you can create a Global Purpose that forms the foundation of your life's service and contribution to the world. For example, my friend Max Avi Kaplan is a talented fashion designer in New York, and he aspires to be distinguished in the highly competitive world of fashion. To gain practice and experience, he worked with several other designers and developed a fashion show to showcase their works. Individuals attending the show were asked to bring canned foods for the local food bank, and the proceeds from the event were donated to nonprofit organizations.

Another person I know has been blessed with the ability to teach others, and he wanted the opportunity to refine and develop this natural gift. To do this, he formed speed-reading courses to help students improve their performance in school. He provided the courses free of charge to students both young and old. The students were amazed at the improvements in their learning and comprehension, and my friend gained experience that helped him choose his next career move.

Other individuals have found their Global Purposes by running for elected public offices or serving on appointed local government boards. I am familiar with several individuals, including a few young adults and students, who have given back to their communities through this type of service, and learned a lot in the process.

So there you have it. I urge you to find a way to serve using your own unique ideas and to play to your strengths. Get other people involved to do the things that you're not good at or need help with. Regardless of your strengths and weaknesses, you can get started on the world problem you've set out to solve.

PART II

CHANGING YOUR LIFE

Service is a spirit in addition to a set of actions. This section explains how you can engineer your life so that your service is as meaningful, fulfilling, and helpful as possible. When serving others is personally gratifying and has a positive effect on your life, you are more likely to continue making a significant impact on the world. This is a newer and more effective way to give, serve, and change our world.

CHAPTER 5

Face Up to Fears

Believing in Yourself, Your Goals, and Your Service

"You gain strength, courage, and confidence by every experience in which you really stop to look fear in the face. You must do the thing which you think you cannot do."
— ELEANOR ROOSEVELT

Overcoming self-doubt is one of the most difficult personal challenges many people face. I have never been blessed with an overwhelming sense of confidence. This really hit home a couple of years ago when I decided to do a research project on members of Congress and their mentors. The main part of the project involved interviewing as many congresspeople as possible, and I was really excited about this. However, when I was walking into a congressman's office for my first interview, I nearly froze with trepidation. To be honest, I was flat out scared. The receptionist led me into the congressman's personal office and asked me to sit down at the end of a long table. I had wanted to do this for a long time, and here was my chance—but I was truly frightened.

There was no rational reason for this: I had thoroughly prepped my questions and done the background research. I actually enjoy speaking in public and was never afraid to ask questions in class. All signs were a go, but I couldn't have been more on edge. I had never conducted an interview before, and the self-doubts were seizing my mind.

Moments later, the congressman walked into the room wearing khaki pants and a casual button-down shirt. He gave me a sideways smile and shook my hand. We did the typical introductions, and I proceeded to ask him about his mentors.

He described his father and told me stories about how they would talk politics at the dinner table. As I continued with the interview, he revealed treasured family histories and memories of the advice he had received from his parents and other mentors. I gradually became more comfortable—the congressman was not nearly as intimating as I had thought he would be, and he even seemed soft-spoken and somewhat shy.

We ended up talking for about an hour instead of the fifteen minutes I had been allotted by his scheduler. Then, as I was wrapping up the interview, the congressman turned the tables by asking me some questions. He wanted to know my thoughts on higher education and what I would change. We talked about the importance of public service and what I was doing with Students Serve. Afterwards, I realized that the interview went better than I had ever envisioned. He even asked me to make a follow-up appointment to tell him the results of the research project. By the time I left, my confidence was soaring.

"One isn't necessarily born with courage,
but one is born with potential. Without courage,
we cannot practice any other virtue with consistency.
We can't be kind, true, merciful, generous, or honest."
— MAYA ANGELOU

GLOBAL PURPOSE AND FEAR

Overcoming your fears can lead to some exciting realizations and life changes, just as it did for me when I interviewed my first member of Congress. Having a Global Purpose is ambitious and can be fear-inspiring, but meeting the goals you set up for yourself will raise your confidence and self-esteem remarkably. Your vision fits into your ambitions and will convince you that you can accomplish the things that you've always wanted to do in your life.

I learned a really valuable lesson during that first congressional interview: One of the hardest parts of doing anything challenging is taking the first step toward making what you want a new reality. For example, think about how many people read books about starting a business, having children, investing, or beginning a new career. They get excited by the prospect of doing something big in their lives, something that will change their world outlook and personal satisfaction dramatically. They want this more than anything else, and believe it would make their lives complete and meaningful.

Yet they never do it. Their dreams are intimidating, so they get scared and back away. They revert to the temporary comfort of living a comfortable life and shove their dreams aside. A few years later, they may realize that they regret their choices, and their lives are still not fulfilling. They have denied themselves what they truly want because they are afraid.

"Courage is not the absence of fear, but rather the judg-
ment that something else is more important than fear."
—AMBROSE REDMOON

"Moral cowardice that keeps us from speaking our minds
is as dangerous to this country as irresponsible talk.
The right way is not always the popular and easy way.
Standing for right when it is unpopular
is a true test of moral character."
—MARGARET CHASE SMITH

If I had decided not to go through with the interview with the member of Congress, I would have lost confidence in my abilities to conduct interviews and to do things that were important to me. Instead, I proved to myself that I could do it. Later, I ended up interviewing more than sixty members of the House and Senate.

If you back away, there is no chance that you will live the life that you want to live. You may never prove to yourself that you are capable of changing the world and improving your life. Your dreams will be just that: dreams. There is no point in complaining about an unfulfilled life or a horrible world if you don't do anything to make your dreams a reality.

That's what your Global Purpose is about. It represents your power to change the things that are wrong with this world and with your life. You have some control over your life, and you can solve global problems. You may start small, but you have the ability make a meaningful impact. In addition, because your vision is tied into your personal goals, accomplishing it will enable you to prove to yourself that you can make your childhood and adult dreams real. Your life can be lived to the fullest if you choose to confront the things you fear.

■

David Chavez

David Chavez has found that service comes in many different forms. It can even have unexpected fringe benefits. In his senior year studying industrial design, David became fascinated by watches—how they worked, their aesthetic beauty, how they could be improved. When he was researching watches online for a final project, he happened to come across some images of timepieces for blind people. He was intrigued by the concept of enabling visually impaired individuals to tell time, but he found that the available designs were archaic and weren't meeting the needs of many blind people.

There were two primary types of watches. One required users to push a button, and the time was audibly announced. The other design required users to feel raised dots that indicated numbers around a clock. These watches frequently did not produce accurate readings of the time. David thought he could make a better watch.

Initially, he had no intentions of turning his senior project into something that could change the world. However, he decided to visit the Blind Institute closest to where he lives in California. He met with professors and other visually impaired individuals to learn about their unique needs and how the current watch designs could be improved. Doing this, he realized that products designed for disabled individuals are often outdated, clumsy, and, quite frankly, unattractive. David thought he could design a watch that was both fashionable and functional.

The result was the Haptica Moveable Braille Timepiece, an innovative watch for the visually impaired that uses Braille numerical dots in a straight channel on the watch face. David's work has not gone unnoticed. He has received international recognition for his work, including a Spark Design Award and a bronze recognition at the International Design Excellence Awards competition. These accomplishments would be impressive for a seasoned veteran of industrial design, but David just finished his degree.

In the future, he hopes to design one or two other products for disabled individuals. He is currently attempting to find funding sponsors so that he can produce the watch he invented. David is using his natural gifts to make products that help others. This makes his passion for industrial design even more rewarding.

■

"You have to have confidence in your ability,
and then be tough enough to follow through."
—ROSALYNN CARTER

FACING YOUR FEAR

There are numerous books, tapes, and other guides about how to get rid of your fear, but I don't believe that fear can ever be eliminated. Fear is the body's natural, biological response to danger, meaning that it is intrinsic to being human.

Instead of trying to make fears go away, I think it is important to do everything possible to minimize these emotions and understand their effects on you. Many times, our brains are irrational, and there really isn't anything to be scared of at all. To manage your fear, you need to learn how to balance the consequences of walking away and having an unfulfilling life with the benefits of accomplishing your vision.

Try asking yourself what the worst possible outcome would be if you immediately stopped everything you were doing and decided to fulfill your life ambitions. Starting that nonprofit, going on that service sabbatical in Africa for six months, quitting your job to start your own business; you would be committing yourself to making it happen. Give yourself some time to think about this. If you were to take the plunge and focus all of your efforts on this one goal, what would be the rock bottom worst thing that could happen to you?

For example, if you commit to going on an extended service sabbatical and ask your supervisor for time off from your job, he might refuse to let you return to work following your service. This seems like a rough consequence, and now you know that you will have to find a new job following your trip. Yet, trying to keep things in perspective, think about the specific steps you would take if you were in this situation. Would it really be the end of the world for you? After looking at your bank account, you might realize that you would have enough savings to manage your expenses for a few months. This could give you enough time necessary to find another job. An alternative would be to find an apartment with lower rent. This might be unpleasant for a while, but at least you would still have a roof over you head.

In addition, although finding a new job may be difficult and stressful, you could handle this situation. In fact, you might even be able to get a better job. This could be an ideal opportunity to grow professionally and find a better career path.

> "Courage is going from failure to failure
> without losing enthusiasm."
> —WINSTON CHURCHILL

Say that you are a young widower in your twenties because your spouse died prematurely due to a type of rare cancer. You might be interested in forming a support group for people whose spouses have passed away. The purpose of the group would be to express your concerns to each other and grieve together. So, to get a grip on your fear, you go online and see if there are any Internet support groups for people who have lost their spouses. Usually these groups are only for older people. You send an email to the leader of one of these groups asking for suggestions about how to start a group specifically for people in their twenties and thirties who have lost their husbands or wives. Once you do this, you will have a head start on doing something that can change the lives of people in need. Hesitating to take that first step only increases the fear.

If you are a college student concerned about the high rates of alcoholism on campus, your first step could be to go online and research this serious issue. The facts are compelling, so you could then take notes on what you learned. The next step would be to type it up in your own words. Then, you could use this as content for a website you create to tell your friends about this issue. You could connect it to your Facebook page and include the true stories of students at your school whose lives have been negatively affected by alcohol abuse.

When trying to manage your fears, decide how big your first steps should be. I like the idea of doing something a bit daring at first, but you should decide for yourself what you should do. Ideally, your action step will be big enough to get you excited and give you confidence to accomplish your vision. Although you may not realize it at the time, taking that first action has also started to change your life. You have begun proving to yourself that you can change the world and that you are a powerful person.

After you make your first move, try listing several other actions that you can take to make your vision a reality. Some may be big and others may be small. If you do not have time to do them today, commit yourself to doing them tomorrow. It's important not to let yourself off the hook by making up excuses, such as lack of time, money, or ability.

Little by little, you will discover that you are managing your fear. You will be doing more than you ever thought you could. You may still get nervous every time you call someone to ask for donations, but you do it anyway. The best part is that afterwards, you feel great about yourself and what you have been able to accomplish.

FIND YOUR CHEERLEADERS

Surround yourself with people who will support and encourage you. You want to be around people who will act as your cheerleaders. They will know how important your vision is and what it will mean to your life once you make it happen. They are there for you with a caring message when you face challenges and will urge you to keep going.

Your friends should be willing to support you in accomplishing your vision. They will lend you their expertise or spend a couple of hours licking envelopes with you. These are true friends, and they will cheer you on even when you want to quit or give up. I once read that you can tell who your true friends are because they are the ones you can call at four in the morning to ask a favor in times of emergency. Who are your true friends? They can help you manage and overcome your fears.

> "If I have lost confidence in myself,
> I have the universe against me."
> —RALPH WALDO EMERSON

MOVING BEYOND EXCUSES

Here are some specific ways you can get past the justifications that keep many of us from changing the world and improving our lives.

Too Inexperienced

If you're just starting out on your own, be careful not to get stuck in the potentially lifelong trap of telling yourself that you don't have enough experience. Try asking yourself when you will be experienced enough. On the eve of your fortieth birthday, will the fact that the clock has struck midnight suddenly mean that you are now an experienced sage who is old enough to do whatever you really want? Or will it simply mean that another day has passed and your age has increased by one year? I do not believe that there is a single point in time when you are finally experienced enough or educated enough or skilled enough to begin something important.

Many people confuse the number of academic degrees someone has with the potential to do something of importance to the world. However, most people learn best by doing, not cramming to memorize facts for an exam. In addition, remember that some of our most successful people have never gone to college. Even if they have, many accomplished people attribute their success to making a commitment to doing something important when they were young. So, the lesson learned is that you are never too young or too old. You can only be too naïve to think that you are.

Too Stressed

Being stressed is often an excuse that people use to rationalize their refusal to commit to their dreams. Pick up almost any magazine and you will likely find an article such as "Ten Tactics to Tackle Stress" or "Stress-Free Ways to Become a New You."

Being stressed or tired all the time is very common. Everybody feels this way at some point, but the real problem here is that you might not actually be tired. Instead, you could be bored because you have denied yourself what you truly want to do with your life.

Think about the people you know. Most of them would probably tell you that they are always exhausted, rushed, or overwhelmed, but there are a few people who are not. These types of people always seem energized and rarely complain about feeling tired. The difference is that they are embracing their life, doing something that truly matters to them. They are excited about the opportunity to live and do the things that are meaningful to them and the people they love.

If you are feeling tired all the time, it may mean that you are doing things that are not truly important to you. If, instead, you decide to focus on something you care about, such as your Global Purpose, you might be amazed at the sudden rush of energy that you get. Of course, you may have to make some difficult decisions about how to use your time, but it will probably be worth it in order to lead a life of meaning and value.

Prioritize Career, Friends, and Family

The importance of careers, friends, and family cannot be emphasized enough. However, *you* are important as well, and your well-being can affect the well-being of your family and your success at work.

Ask yourself when you are the best friend, brother, sister, parent, or aunt possible. It's probably not when you've had a bad day at work or traffic was backed up for hours or you were working on something that wasn't interesting to you. More likely, it's when you nail that important presentation at work, get home early due to no traffic jams, or are working on something exciting. That's when you are best with your friends and family. It's because you are content.

Making your vision happen will enable you to become satisfied with yourself and your lifestyle. You can transfer this inner satisfaction to other areas in your life, and it will make you a better employee, business owner, friend, father, mother, or son. Valuing yourself and honoring your personal needs will improve the lives of the other people around you.

Too Old

Even though I am still in my twenties, I find that I sometimes make excuses because I feel as if I'm too old. I know this may seem crazy, but it's true. It seems like the world is full of child prodigies, nineteen-year-old millionaires, and people like Mary Kate and Ashley Olsen, who were acting practically since birth. Whether you are young or old, you can let yourself believe the myth that you are a late bloomer and that your time has passed. However, it is important to remember that some of the most influential people throughout history did not get started on their dreams and Global Purposes until they were well past middle age. For example, Clara Barton founded the American Red Cross when she was sixty years old. Colonel Sanders started Kentucky Fried Chicken when he was sixty-six. Mary Kay Ash started her nationwide cosmetics company, Mary Kay, when she was forty-five. These are just a few examples of people who did not make excuses for their lives because they believed they were too old to succeed.

Try asking yourself two simple questions. If not now, when? Have you gone through your life excusing yourself away from what would be meaningful? Decide today that you will live the life you always dreamed of when you were just starting out and got your first job. It's time to wake up and finally live.

"Don't be too timid and squeamish about your actions.
All life is an experiment.
The more experiments you make, the better."
—RALPH WALDO EMERSON

CHAPTER 6

Meaningful Money

Using Your Money to Make a Difference

"Lack of money is the root of all evil."
— GEORGE BERNARD SHAW

"Make money your god and it will
plague you like the devil."
— HENRY FIELDING

Money is important for changing your world and your life. It
costs something to start a nonprofit organization, send clothes to
impoverished children, or form a website to create a forum for
family members to communicate about a loved one's rare disease. It also costs something to put food on your own table, pay
the rent, save for retirement, and clothe yourself. Both are important. It is important to find the right balance between them
if you want to have a healthy view of money and to increase your
ability to change the world.

Go ahead and take a second glance at the two quotes above.
They couldn't be more different about the virtues/vices of money.

No wonder society has such conflicting views about the role it should play in our lives! On the one hand, money's just a way for us to purchase the things we need to live. On the other hand, it can make people greedy and keep them from caring about the things in life that truly matter.

Numerous businesses, marketers, banks, politicians, financial advisors, and family members try to influence how you view money and what you choose to spend it on. However, it is important to decide for yourself the role that money will play in your life. To some people, money is important because it can represent the ability to live in security. To others, it can represent freedom and independence. And to others, money can create a peace of mind or sense of comfort. These are all important values, and everyone is different. Because of this, I have found that it is important for everyone to define for themselves how they feel about material wealth by thinking through and answering the following questions.

- What does money mean to you? (Security, freedom, the ability to buy things, peace of mind, power . . . ?)
- How much money do you want?
- How much money do you need?
- What do you want to do with the money you make?
- Is wealth the most important thing in your life?
- Are you in debt?
- Do you have too much money? (Yes, this is possible!)
- Does extreme frugality harm your relationships with others?

- Do you obsess over getting wealthy?
- Is it hard for you to give money away to others?

> "Make all you can, save all you can, give all you can."
> —JOHN WESLEY

MONEY AND HAPPINESS

Money can buy things and experiences that make us happy. No honest person would deny that using money to buy a new house, fabulous car, or those red shoes at the mall can put a smile on your face and make you feel good about your life. Having the money necessary to buy these things makes you feel good about yourself, at least temporarily. This indicates that there is a definite connection between money and happiness. In addition, the lack of money can make people unhappy when they are unable to meet their needs. Having basic food, clothing, and shelter is necessary to live, and having enough money to pay for these things is vital. So there is certainly a relationship between money and happiness.

However, I do not believe that money in and of itself is happiness. There are many wealthy people who are miserable and hate their lives. The recent suicides of investors and corporate traders are tragic reminders that money cannot necessarily buy a good life.

Some people, whether they are rich or poor, are deluded into believing that having money and using it to buy things will make their lives full of meaning and personal satisfaction. They will pay almost any price to buy the cars, jewelry, clothes, food, and anything else they think will give them satisfaction. Unfortunately, they are missing the mark every time they pull out their credit cards. The reason for this is that things do not have lasting personal meaning or value. Having a car that costs as much as a house, for example, is only an *outward* symbol of wealth. As clichéd as it may sound, I have found that true wealth is found on the inside, in your soul. Possessions can only make you appear to be rich, successful, and happy. They cannot enrich your soul.

I urge you to take a closer look at where your money goes each month. Are you spending it in ways that make you happy? What areas do you need to spend more on in order to maximize your enjoyment in life? In order to do or have those things, what do you need to spend less on?

This is not about saving every cent that you make and sending all of your clothes to impoverished people around the world. It is about using your money well, using it to provide for the needs of yourself and others. It's possible that you spend more than you need to and that a lot of your money is going toward things that you do not find fulfilling.

This can even be the case if you're not in debt and aren't extravagant. For example, I have clothes in my closet that have never been worn. Sure, I got great deals on them, but they're just hanging there. This is wasteful. It is a sign that I do not always spend money in ways that match what my values are. I also have food in my pantry that I probably will not eat. I have movies that I never watch, books I never read, makeup I've never opened. The list could go on. I'm not a big spender, and I'm fortunate that I'm not swimming in debt, but I could still improve the ways I use money. This is something we all need to work on, and reviewing your spending can help.

Here's a strategy that I've found to be helpful. When you're in the store about to buy something, most people tell you to think about whether or not you really need it. If that approach doesn't work for you, you might ask yourself if you could buy something else with the money that would make your life more valuable.

Think about it this way:

Which would have a more important impact on your life, spending $70 on another new pair of shoes or on launching the website that would enable you to fulfill your vision of providing books to children?

Which would be more personally satisfying, a $2,200 to vacation in the Outer Banks with your family or a $2,400 family trip to provide medical services to people in Guatemala? Which would you likely remember longer?

Would spending $15 to get your hair cut at the cheap stylist be worth it if you could take the $60 you saved by not going to your usual salon and use it to buy stamps and envelopes to send out letters encouraging people to recycle their garbage?

If you really want that pair of shoes and know that you would wear them at least several times a week for the next year, go ahead and buy them. If launching the new website is important to you as well, then figure out another way to make it happen. There is a solution to every problem.

> "An object in possession seldom retains
> the same charm that it had in pursuit."
> —PLINY THE YOUNGER

MAKE IT HURT

Giving money to others can be deeply personal. For some people, making donations seems to come as second nature. To these individuals, it just seems like the right thing to do, especially when they have been blessed with plenty to eat and a place to call home. For others, giving requires effort and doesn't come easily. As my history with tithing indicates, I definitely fall into the category of people who have a more difficult time parting with money, regardless of how fortunate I may be.

If you have not gotten into the habit of setting aside some of your income for others, the best way to do this is to start small. At first, try giving as much as you can without feeling like your lifestyle is dramatically changing. Once you do this, you will realize how painless giving to others can be and how personally gratifying it can make you feel. Then, increase how much you give each month. You may decide to cut back on some of your unnecessary spending so that you can give as much as you think you should. However, when you make tradeoffs, your gifts will matter not only to others but to you. You don't have to give, but you choose to. That is empowering, and even life changing.

Giving away money can make your job more meaningful and fulfilling, too. Working long hours in a corporate environment can be tiresome, and many people have started to question if they should quit and work for the government or a nonprofit to do "good." Others have decided that they must strike out on their own and start their own business in order to find value in their work. However, when you know that a portion of your salary will be donated to a worthy cause, this can help you appreciate your current job situation. Just because you work at a for-profit business doesn't mean that you are not contributing to society. The better you are at your job, the more money you can make, and the more money you can give away to others.

> "The ideals which have lighted my way, and time after time have given me new courage to face life cheerfully, have been Kindness, Beauty, and Truth. The trite subjects of possessions, outward success, luxury have always seemed to me contemptible."
> —ALBERT EINSTEIN

DONATION NATION

- $233 billion—the amount in charitable donations given by Americans each year
- 54 percent—the percentage of donations given to nonprofits that were kept by fundraising corporations, not charities, according to a *Los Angeles Times* investigation of over 5,800 nonprofit fundraising campaigns
- 92 percent—the percentage of Americans who make donations to nonprofit organizations

If you're like most Americans, you give away a portion of your income to charities, church, or other nonprofit organizations. It gives you a good feeling to be able to support the local firefighters who call in the middle of dinner or to drop a few coins in the red Salvation Army bucket at Christmas. You probably try to capitalize on that nice tax deduction you get from the IRS as well.

Although giving away money is admirable, do you actually know where your donations are going? Would you give your retirement savings to a financial planner who sends you a nice letter asking to invest your funds for a fee without asking about his experience? I certainly hope not!

Yet this is essentially what most people do with their donation dollars. They get a nice letter from a local nonprofit organization telling about sick children and asking for money. The problem is that you have no idea where your money is going.

Donations are investments in a better world.

Investing in a Better World

The goal for making your donations count as much as possible is to put your money where it will generate the most value and have the largest impact on improving society.

In this sense, think like the great investor Warren Buffett. Mr. Buffett has consistently beaten the stock market by huge margins. Basically, his primary strategy has been to invest in a small number of companies that he was nearly certain would be really profitable. Unlike most Wall Street investors who spread their money around, buying portions of hundreds or thousands of companies, he has concentrated his funds in the places where they could give the biggest return. The strategy has paid off, and he is usually listed as one of the top three richest people in the world.

Buffett applied this same concept to donating his fortunes. Instead of spreading it around to hundreds of thousands of different charities he knew nothing about, he pledged the majority of his funds to one organization, the Bill and Melinda Gates Foundation. He knew the founders well, and after talking with them, he became confident that they would spend his money wisely. They were interested in solving social problems, not just administering temporary fixes.

Follow Warren Buffet's lead. Pick out several organizations that interest you. You may have learned about them when researching your vision, through your church, TV shows, or the newspaper, or they may have sent you letters. Go to their websites. Look to see what strategies they are using. Are they actually solving the problem they say they are solving? Or are they simply providing a quick fix?

There are several websites that provide ratings for nonprofit organizations and let you look at their tax filings for the year. Each nonprofit above a certain size is required to submit a form to the IRS listing all of their revenues and personnel expenditures. It's called Form 990, and it's a good idea to take a look at it before sending any money. Check out these two websites: Guidestar (*www.guidestar.org*) and Charity Navigator (*www.charitynavigator.org*).

The "Five Whys" that you used earlier to find the root cause for your Global Purpose may be useful here as well. Ask yourself why you think the problem exists until you narrow down some of the causes for the problem: Why children are starving, why there are homeless people on the streets, why there are no service grants for college students.

If an organization is addressing these issues, it's likely to be a good place for you to invest your donation dollars. Compare the organizations and pick the one recipient you believe will use your funds most effectively. Remember, it's best not to split your donation and give to multiple organizations. Give to the organization that you think will put your money to the best use.

It's important that you do not discount your donations as being too small. Every small amount of money helps, and it really adds up when lots of people give.

"One must be poor to know the luxury of giving."
— GEORGE ELIOT

CHAPTER 7

The Time of Your Life

Maximizing Your Time on Earth

"You must give some time to your fellow men. Even if
it's a little thing, do something for others—something for
which you get no pay but the privilege of doing it."

—ALBERT SCHWEITZER

■

Carla Harris

If Carla Harris can make time to serve others, anyone can. During
the day (and frequently after dark), she works at a high-powered investment bank as managing director in the Strategic Client Group in
New York City. In this role, she helps corporations raise millions of
dollars in public and private equity capital. Yet despite the demands
of an intense career, Carla has flourished by finding a way to give
others the same opportunities she has been fortunate to have.

Outside work, Carla is a gifted gospel singer who frequently
performs in churches and schools. She's performed at Carnegie

Hall, sung with gospel legends, and recorded multiple CDs. Through her performances and the sales of her recordings, Carla has been able to donate more than $250,000 to scholarship funds at two high schools in her native Jacksonville, Florida. She feels very privileged to have had the chance to go to one of the best schools in her hometown. And now, she is providing similar opportunities to other students.

Establishing the scholarships has offered her a way keep connected with her roots. Carla continues to stay in touch with many of the recipients of the scholarships and acts as a mentor. In addition, she helps govern and lead several nonprofit organizations as a member of their boards of directors. She finds that the immediate feedback of helping others is very gratifying. Her parents were exemplary servants, and she has intentionally made service an important part of her life as well.

When asked about how she gets everything done, she said that she aggressively guards her calendar. She uses her time to do the things that matter most to her, and she strategically limits other nonessential obligations and time commitments. As a result, she has been able to pursue gospel singing, her passion in life, and help others.

Working long hours in a demanding career has never stopped Carla. The scholarships provide a way for hardworking yet underprivileged students to get a good education. They also give Carla a way to stay grounded amidst the intense and money-immersed Wall Street environment. Service keeps her focused on what is truly important and enables her to live an active and fulfilling life.

■

As you change your world, it is inevitable that you are going to add things to your already packed to-do list. We all feel over-whelmed at times, especially when we think of adding extra commitments. This chapter will help you learn how to use your time so that everything that's important to you gets done. You will even have time to rest.

TIME IS LIFE

I believe that whoever said that "time is money" was wrong. Think about it. Your time is your life. All of the seconds form all of the minutes which form all of the hours which form all of the days, months, and years that make up your life. Time is life. Value it, cherish it, and use it well. If you waste your time, you waste your life.

It's crucial to make sure that you spend your time doing the things you love. I'm not necessarily advocating that you abdicate all of your responsibilities and go take an eighteen-month trip to Aruba. If that's how you want to spend your time and you can afford it, that's great. Rather, I'm referring to the time that we spend every day at work, watching TV, going out with family and friends, buying groceries, paying bills, and doing all of the things we think we "have" to do.

Balancing all of our responsibilities in life is a constant chal-lenge. How frequently do you hear yourself or the people around you say that they're "running out of time," "pressed for time," "in need of more time," "just too busy," or "flat out exhausted"? It seems like we are always complaining about a lack of time. We have so much to do, and we can never seem to fit everything into our busy schedules. However, it is possible to form a strategy that enables you to use your time in a way that gives you the most satisfaction out of life.

What important things have you said no to because you felt like you didn't have enough time?

Did you regret your decisions later? If not, will you regret them in the future?

Your time is your life. Have you been wasting your life?

"How wonderful it is that nobody need wait a single moment before starting to improve the world."
—ANNE FRANK

TIME CHECK

Even if you haven't been making the best use of your time, you can change this. The best way to start is to go through your day and think about how you spend your time. It might be helpful to write it all down on paper. This is what I did when first beginning to form a strategy for using my time well. On a piece of paper, I wrote down everything I did for an entire day, from waking up and going for my morning run to turning off the light before bed. On the left-hand side, I wrote the time that I started doing each activity. It's a bit tedious, but what you learn will likely surprise you.

Among other things, I realized that I took over an hour to eat dinner each night. That's a long time spent eating. Summed up over a week, that equals more than seven hours eating dinner, nearly all of the productive working hours of a whole day. I also learned that I spend a lot of time getting dressed and ready for work each morning. I don't get much satisfaction out of eating long dinners or taking a long time to get dressed. I realized that I really was not using my time well. I really was not using my *life* well.

There were so many other things I would have preferred to do. I wanted to send out press releases for Students Serve, go out with friends, write a new fundraising letter, read a new book. Before, I thought that I didn't have enough time to do any of these things.

Fortunately, by learning how I was spending my time each day, I have been able to make some modifications and fit in some of these other things that are really important to me. Instead of taking thirty minutes to pick out an outfit, put on makeup, get my stuff together, and head out the door, I decided one day that I would try to do it all in twenty minutes. I would use the remaining ten minutes to outline the fundraising letter. In fact, I was actually able to get ready in ten minutes, a third of the time it took me to get ready the day before. Just by thinking about how I used my time enabled me to get something done that I had thought impossible. I had a full twenty minutes to work on the fundraising letter. This may seem simplistic, but it has really worked for me.

TIME MAXIMIZATION

There are several ways to strategize how you use your time and life, and many of these suggestions involve a change in your frame of mind. This type of mindfulness was the reason I was able to painlessly reduce the time I spent getting ready in the mornings. Intentionally using your time in a way that is meaningful is much more effective than adding complex systems of multiple planners, calendars, and timers. The goal is to enjoy your life, not to rush through it.

When you're just getting started on this, it's probably best to read through the strategies and pick the ones that seem to match your lifestyle and goals. I think it's a good idea to implement only one or two at a time because if you try too many, you may become overwhelmed. It's ironic, but it's possible to waste a lot of time trying to manage your time.

> "We have many items on our plates at all times as judges.
> I can only work on one at a time, and when I work on one,
> I give it my full attention, and I do the best I can with it.
> Then I go on to something else."
> —SANDRA DAY O'CONNOR

ACCEPTING YOUR HUMANNESS

You can do anything, but you can't do everything. This concept is just like choosing a cause to focus on, and it is one of the most important principles in learning how to use your time well. When you formed your Global Purpose, you selected the one most important way to change the world. You did not try to figure out how you could promote minority rights, find a cure for multiple sclerosis, and preserve clean drinking water. Instead, you identified the one thing that was most important to you in an area in which you could make a meaningful difference.

Even though you might not have realized this at the time, you were channeling your inner Al Gore, Rachael Ray, or any other successful person. Al Gore set one overarching goal for himself—to preserve the environment. This has played a key role in his success. He concentrated his efforts on one thing. He was not trying to educate others about fossil fuel emissions while simultaneously starting a Fortune 500 company, trying to become the next Heisman trophy winner, and creating a 27th letter in the alphabet. Instead, he focused his time on trying to save the environment.

Rachael Ray is another example of this. She uses her time to become the best celebrity quick-meal chef she can be. She doesn't spread her efforts around trying to do everything she wants to at the same time. Yes, she has expanded her responsibilities by starting a talk show, a magazine, and a nonprofit organization, but each of these are centered upon her primary goal. Her talk show features her quick cooking segments and family time around the kitchen table. Her magazine, *Every Day with Rachael Ray*, is all about eating, and her nonprofit organization teaches kids how to choose nutritious meals and gives them cooking lessons.

Think about any other successful person, and you will probably find that the same is true. These individuals pick out one or two specific goals and use their time to accomplish them. They channel their energy into these issues despite having other interests because they know that once they are successful at one thing, they can propel that success, self-confidence, and experience into accomplishing their other goals.

Think about all of your commitments and eliminate the obligations that are not contributing to your success at work or home. This is easier said than done, but it's almost always necessary in order to make time for the things that give your life meaning and fulfillment.

THE END TO PERFECTIONISM

At first, setting the highest possible standards for yourself seems like a good thing. However, you must also accept that you are physically and mentally incapable of achieving perfection in everything. Excellence and perfection are two very different and often confused concepts. We should all strive for excellence and leave perfection behind.

Go for greatness, but only in the things that matter to you. By now you've picked out the things you really care about doing. Do them well. Strive for excellence in those things but in nothing else. Do your best in all of your other commitments *given the time you've got.* It is important to accept that some things can be "good enough" and that you can do them well but not perfectly.

BARE BASICS

Before I began periodically reviewing how I spent my time, I did a lot of things that added little benefit to my health or happiness. I just did them because I thought I had to. I realized that many of the obligations we think we have to fulfill are not actually compulsory.

For example, ever since I learned to read, I've spent a great deal of time reading almost all of the newspaper in order to get a full grip on the news. It seemed like the right thing to do to be an informed citizen. However, as admirable as that may have seemed, by lunchtime, I couldn't even remember half the things I had read. Now, I usually skim the front-page and local sections and then read through the opinion page, but that's it. A side benefit is that I remember more of what I read each morning because my mind isn't overwhelmed with useless information.

Go through your planner or to-do list and think through your schedule. What habits can you change to free up time and accomplish your goals?

> "Don't be the slave of your inbox. Just because some-
> thing's there doesn't mean you have to do it."
> —MALCOLM FORBES SR.

JACKSON POLLOCK PLANNER

When I reached the fifth grade, my teachers told my classmates and I that we were expected to use an assignment planner. We were told to write down everything we wanted to remember to do for that day, and to note important deadlines/events that were coming up.

A planner is an amazing time-management tool. I only wish they had taught me how to use it effectively! In high school, the planner requirement had served me well. However, during college, my planner began looking somewhat like a Jackson Pollock painting, with scribbled notes, events, and to-do lists in different colors everywhere. My weeks were planned well in advance. Friday was filled with things to do even though it was only Monday.

I was overwhelmed. Fortunately, I found a solution by writing a list of the things I wanted to do only one day ahead of time in my planner. Now, I don't write out my life six days in advance. One day is enough. I can handle this, and it is manageable. The biggest benefit is that I no longer worry about everything I have to get done for the rest of the week. Instead, I can focus my attention on striving for excellence one day at a time. I continue to record meetings in my planner so that I don't double-book, but that's it. I take it one day at a time.

I also limit my daily list to about five or six objectives. I have learned that this is usually all that I will realistically be able to get done in a day. Other things will inevitably come up that waste my time, and I try to limit them as much as possible. But by concentrating on my daily list, I have confidence and know that I can get these tasks done. I list them in order of importance and start in the morning with the item that's top on the list. If the bottom things don't get done, that's okay.

At the end of the day, if I haven't completed everything I wanted to get done, I simply put the unfinished tasks on tomorrow's block in my planner. Eventually, I get everything done in a timely manner, which also helps me manage stress. And even though I occasionally get overwhelmed, I'm usually able to focus on the things that are most important so that I do them as well as possible—without a breakdown.

REST

I do not believe in wasting time. However, I always try to set aside time most days of every week to rest. Reading an interesting book, watching a favorite show, and going for walks at daybreak are my favorite ways to relax. I've discovered that without enough time to rest, I simply can't do anything else. My body literally shuts down. I sit for hours in front of my laptop trying to do work and end up with nothing worthwhile. At some point, I learned that I have to stop.

Take the time to rest.

Once I give my mind and body a chance to be still and rest, I amaze myself with increased productivity. It might take me only ten minutes to finish the second half of a Students Serve press release when the first half took me over an hour. After some time to relax, my energy levels bounce up again.

GET ENTHUSIASTIC

If you're really enthusiastic about something, the time will fly by. Your energy level will skyrocket, and you will get more work done than you ever though possible. It may seem surprising, but the time spent doing this will not matter. Doing something that seems impossible is daunting at first, but once you take the first step, you will be hooked. You'll get into "the zone." Nothing will interrupt your thoughts, and you will be concentrating completely on what you're doing because it is important to you. When you're finished, you will not believe what you have done and how little time it took.

Get enthusiastic. You will find that you can make the time to fit it into your busy schedule.

> "The reasonable man adapts himself to the world;
> the unreasonable one persists in trying to
> adapt the world to himself. Therefore all
> progress depends on the unreasonable man."
> — GEORGE BERNARD SHAW

GET HELP!

When first starting Students Serve, I realized that in order to raise money I was going to have to get the word out about what I wanted to do. There was no way around it. I had to get Students Serve featured in newspapers. This would help with fundraising and it would enable me to prove my credibility and dedication to the organization. The prospect of being in the newspaper was exciting.

The problem was that I had no idea how to do this. From some preliminary online research, I realized that I would first have to write a press release, essentially writing a newspaper article about Students Serve and why it was newsworthy. I went ahead and wrote up what I thought was a decent press release and sent it to local reporters.

I got no response. I waited two more weeks. Still no response. Eventually, I brought in the pros. I asked a public relations expert at my college for help, and she completely rewrote the press release for me. She sent the release to local papers, and within a couple of weeks, Students Serve was in a feature story.

I could not have done this on my own. If you're not an expert in something and don't have the time to learn how to become one, ask for help. Many people will be interested in knowing what you're doing. They're even likely be willing to give you some of their time and advice for free. I have gotten expert advice from professional fundraising consultants, nonprofit executives, publicity experts, and other people who know what they're talking about. All you have to do is ask for help.

Congressman Tom Perriello

When I caught up with Congressman Perriello, he had just come back from a Saturday morning run. That weekend, he would be attending an annual retreat for members of Congress, and being able to participate in this event was the natural next step in answering his life calling. Tom Perriello, one of the youngest members of Congress, feels as though he has been called to service.

As a part of what is being labeled the community service generation, he grew up learning how to give to others. He was a Boy Scout and was actively involved in church activities in the community. In college, he tutored other students and became active in environmentalism. After graduating from law school, Perriello turned down lucrative career opportunities in order to devote his life to service by addressing world problems. He worked in ravaged areas of Liberia and Sierra Leone to help bring an end to the violence and destruction that were the result of years of civil wars. In an effort to bring reconciliation to the people of these countries, he helped promote pro-democracy groups and worked to give children and amputees a voice in the peace talks.

He then worked as a Special Advisor for the International Prosecutor, helping in an effort to oust a Liberian dictator from power without violent force. Perriello was excited about what his service was helping to accomplish. He loved what he was doing because he knew the significance of his work, and he felt personally blessed to be involved in these efforts and living out his life calling. "I woke up ecstatic about what I was doing every day. I couldn't imagine doing anything else." After returning to the United States, he helped start several faith-based organizations and acted as a national security analyst.

In 2007, Perriello decided to broaden the scope of his service work from community service to public service. Displeased by both the Democratic and Republican candidates campaigning for congressional office, he decided to enter the race and offer a fresh alternative. He believed that his on-the-ground experience with service could provide a new and valuable perspective in Congress.

Before beginning the campaign, Perriello decided that he would run for office on his own terms. Service formed a primary part of the campaign vision that he communicated to voters. His campaign staff and volunteers practiced "volunteer tithing," on which they spent 10 percent of their time working on projects for nonprofit organizations and other community groups instead of handing out fliers door to door and making fundraising calls.

In one of the most closely watched and hotly contested elections in 2008, Perriello defeated an entrenched incumbent congressman by only 727 votes. This defeat was one of the biggest upsets of the election, and Congressman Perriello believes that the way he ran the campaign, emphasizing his background in service and the importance of volunteering, made the difference.

Now, as a member of Congress, Perriello views himself and the group of other newly elected members as part of a Public Service Generation. Many of these individuals come to Congress with experience serving in the community and are now passionate about institutionalizing the changes they were able to make on a local scale so that communities across the nation can benefit. On a personal level, for Perriello this represents a chance to continue living out his lifetime call to service.

CHAPTER 8

A Fulfilling Life

Living Your Legacy

"Every day you may make progress. Every step may be
fruitful. Yet there will stretch out before you an
ever-lengthening, ever-ascending, ever-improving path.
You know you will never get to the end of the journey.
But this, so far from discouraging, only adds
to the joy and glory of the climb."
—WINSTON CHURCHILL

Aunt Betty Lynn is one of my favorite people in the world. When
I was younger and my family and I visited Arkadelphia, Arkansas,
to see her, she always gave my sister and me "surprises." Bright
red lipstick, a new hair brush, a new box of colored pencils—she
had a surprise for each day of our visit.

My sister Ginny and I thought this was the best thing ever.
The surprises were usually fun toys and trinkets. But the gifts
themselves were not what we loved. It was our aunt's thoughtful-
ness that was so special. We would spend hours playing "beauty
parlor," during which she would fix our hair and let us put on her

makeup. We would dress up in fancy clothes for "tea parties" in the dining room, eating the special cucumber finger sandwiches we had made together earlier in the day. Why couldn't all family members be this much fun and so caring? All of my friends knew about Aunt Betty Lynn, and after meeting her, they loved her, too.

As a girl, I remember noticing how differently Aunt Betty Lynn approached the world compared to everyone else I knew. She had a unique zest for life that was infectious. Whenever we would go shopping, she treated everyone in the store as if they were her closest friends. Striking up conversations at the register about the sales clerk's daughter was common. (Sometimes this even meant spending twenty minutes in the checkout line talking with the grocery-store baggers.)

This was more than Southern Hospitality or being a friendly neighbor. Aunt Betty Lynn truly loves other people because they are people. When you're with her, you sense that you are the most important person on Earth. She makes you believe that you are truly matchless and invaluable.

My aunt is living her legacy. Through her service work and her unique approach to life, she is living the life that she wants to be remembered for. This is her way of giving to others and fulfilling her own need for happiness. Not only does she make others feel important, her way of living has enriched her days with positivity—despite financial difficulties and health problems, my aunt is the most optimistic person I know. Instead of complaining about her situation, she takes pleasure in the smallest things. This could be baking cookies (and eating the dough!), buying surprises, going on walks, or visiting a neighbor. She has realized that it is the seemingly insignificant things in life that enrich our days with meaning and enable us to live happily. She is someone who will be remembered and cherished long after her time on Earth has come to an end.

> "Never forget that the purpose for which a man lives is
> the improvement of the man himself, so that he may go
> out of this world having, in his great sphere or
> his small one, done some little good for his f
> ellow creatures and labored a little to diminish
> the sin and sorrow that are in the world."
> —WILLIAM E. GLADSTONE

FINDING JOY NOW

So many of us think that change or happiness or excellence can only be achieved at some future time—when we are smarter, more experienced, have a family, buy a boat, build a new house. But once we have the things that we have always wanted or done the things that we have always wanted to do, our lives can still ring hollow.

Happiness is not five years or a new house away. It is right now. It's how you choose to approach every day. Think optimistically. Find the good things that make life worth living. For Aunt Betty Lynn, joy is found in teaching a "slow" student how to read, laughing with grandchildren, calling a friend.

Service is a spirit as well as an action. Along with going on a service sabbatical or starting a website, it is the way you interact with people on a daily basis that will add richness to your life.

Appreciate the wonders of the Earth, the people you are blessed to meet, and the chance to be alive and change the world. These things are worth living for. Love them, cherish them every day. When you wake up each morning, make a conscious choice to embrace the opportunity you have been given to live. Nothing could be greater.

EVERYDAY GREATNESS

Greatness is achieved one day at a time. Fred Rogers, the creator of the television show *Mr. Roger's Neighborhood,* aspired to attain a degree in theology. The majority of his days were already scheduled with tapings for his shows and public appearances. However, he made the time to get his degree by taking a class each day during his lunch break. It took him about eight years, but every day he attended his one class, and eventually he earned the degree.

You make your vision of a better world come into being with your everyday actions. Changing the world does not happen in a single instance. Sure, when you mail out your one thousandth awareness letter or receive thousands of dollars in donations, you may feel as though you have made your impact on the world. But these days are just milestones that represent the culmination of your daily efforts. These are times for celebration, but the actual world changes occurred days, weeks, or months ago.

It is in your everyday choices about how you use your time and money that you make your vision happen and change the world. The same is true for your life. You do not go to bed one night fluent only in English and wake up the next morning speaking Mandarin, Portuguese, Greek, and Russian. You change your life by changing your daily behavior. You decide to learn twenty new Russian words each day. Over time, you become fluent.

> "I expect to pass through this world but once; any good
> thing therefore that I can do, or any kindness that I can
> show to any fellow creature, let me do it now; let me not
> defer or neglect it, for I shall not pass this way again."
> —ETTIENE DE GRELLET

■

The Man on Hogan Road

Finding joy in the midst of everyday life and sharing it with others is crucial to leading a happy life. I will never forget driving down Hogan Road in Nashville each week when I was growing up. Without fail, on just about every sunny day, a man who was mentally handicapped would sit in a lawn chair in his front yard and wave to everyone who drove past. His smile was brilliant, and it almost never failed to make me smile as well. He always seemed so excited to see you drive by. Despite his disability, he had the capability to make others happy. He shared his joy for life with others. And all it took was a big-hearted wave.

■

"Never discourage anyone . . . who continually
makes progress, no matter how slow."
— Plato

ENCOURAGE OTHERS

Another simple, yet surprisingly powerful, way to magnify your impact on the world is to encourage others to serve. Share your experiences and be candid about what service has meant to you personally. They might be convinced to do the same.

Think of the potential influence this can have on the world. Instead of griping about the latest break-in or war, people will do something to address the problems we face. They will take matters into their own hands just as you have and will improve the world. Their efforts might be small. It's possible that yours will be, too. But when all of our efforts are combined, the impact is significant. Our world will really change.

Help them as they start to make their vision happen. The easier it is for them to get started, the quicker they will be able to make a meaningful difference. This is not a competition. There should be no rewards for who has the best vision or who is able to feed the most children. The only thing that matters is that we are doing something, we are doing what we can. Lift up others, and they will use their talents to improve the world.

"The universal brotherhood of man
is our most precious possession."
— Mark Twain

CONNECT WITH OTHERS

By living your everyday life and enacting your Global Purpose, you will come into contact with thousands of people. Do not let them slip away unnoticed. People are the most important assets our world has. The whole purpose of changing your world is to make it better for other people and for yourself. It's not just because it's the "right thing to do" or because community service is fun. By reducing fossil fuels, for example, you will help preserve the environment and humans will be able to live on Earth for years to come.

As focused as you may be on making your vision a reality, take the time to form relationships with the people around you. Your life will be better and so will theirs. These bonds with others will make accomplishing your vision even more meaningful and important. These are the people that you are working for.

> "Change has a considerable psychological impact
> on the human mind. To the fearful it is threatening
> because it means that things may get worse.
> To the hopeful it is encouraging because things
> may get better. To the confident it is inspiring
> because the challenge exists to make things better."
> —KING WHITNEY JR.

VALUE YOURSELF

Your value is not determined by the lines on your resume or the number of cars in your garage. You are valuable just by the virtue of being human. In a world in which everything is ranked from best to worst, we often get this confused. Employer reviews, test scores, and bank account figures do not determine your worth.

As you go throughout your day, you talk to yourself. You may not think of it like this, but in your head, there is a voice that gives you instant feedback on everything you do. Pay attention to what you are telling yourself. Is the message positive and encouraging, or do you constantly tell yourself that someone else could have done a better job?

If you forget to pick up the takeout after work one day, does your inner voice tell you that you are forgetful or lazy? If so, this is a problem. It means that you do not value yourself and are constantly putting yourself down. All humans forget things. It just happens. By tearing yourself apart for something that is ultimately trivial, you are forcing yourself to live up to unrealistic, unachievable standards. You are subconsciously telling yourself that you have to do more and be better than anyone else in order to be acceptable.

Make an intentional effort to always praise yourself. At first, this seems annoyingly positive and optimistically vain. However, you will realize that it makes an enormous difference to how you view yourself. When you can't remember where you put your keys, you will forgive yourself. It's okay. It's not the end of the world.

You will also keep things in perspective. At least you have keys. These keys unlock a car or a place to live. Many people around the globe have neither. In the scheme of your life and the world, losing your keys does not matter at all. Let yourself off the hook here. Is it still frustrating? Sure. But you are accepting that some things just happen. If you don't, you will never be willing to take a chance on changing your world and your life. If you beat yourself up over misplacing your keys, why would you allow yourself to solve a world problem? You've got to get over this. Let yourself live. You are human, too.

> "Twenty years from now you will be more
> disappointed by the things that you didn't do than
> by the ones you did do. So throw off the bowlines.
> Sail away from the safe harbor. Catch the trade
> winds in your sails. Explore. Dream. Discover."
> —MARK TWAIN

REINVENT YOURSELF

There will come a time when you need to make a life change, and this doesn't just mean going blond or throwing out your favorite oversized college sweatshirt. This is a big change that will reshape your life into something totally different. It may be starting a business, getting married, going on an adventurous vacation, starting a new job, or anything else that will throw a curve into your current lifestyle.

This is true for your Global Purpose as well. Organizing a march to protest deforestation takes guts. So does starting a non-profit or changing careers or going back to school. All of these things will change your life and how you think of yourself and the world.

Right before you take the jump is the scariest time of all. It's like looking over a cliff and not knowing what's down below you. It is unknown and frightening. You are tempted to back away, to return to that area of your life that you have already conquered. But if you are honest with yourself, you know that this will lead to unfulfillment. Inside your soul, you know that you must change. As much as you want the change, you fear it as well. It is new, unknown, and intimidating.

Do not ignore these fears. Listen to them. That is the only way you will get past them. Do anything you need to do in order to convince yourself that the change is possible. Then go do it. Just do it. Reinvent yourself. Make the life change that will enable you to live the life you have always wanted to live.

CELEBRATE

One thing we do not do frequently enough in life is celebrate our successes. When you do something good, praise yourself and other people. You've worked hard. Appreciate everything you've done and enjoy the personal satisfaction that comes from changing your world. You have just proven that you are powerful. The world is not doomed to failure or misery. You can make it better. You can change the world. Reward yourself. Go out for ice cream. You'll be much more likely to keep up the wonderful work you're doing and have reason to celebrate again in the future.

GIVING AND TRULY LIVING

When people say that they want to live a fulfilling life, they often mean that they want to do something important, to not live their lives in vain. When we see all of the wretched images on TV and in the paper, we feel overwhelmed and powerless. How can we let these things happen? Our lives seem insignificant and we feel helpless. This feeling of powerlessness leads to dissatisfaction with our lives and questions about why we are even on this Earth to begin with.

Yet there is hope. As you will see and experience, giving your time and talent to others can make a meaningful difference in solving world problems. You can change the world. You are not powerless. At the same time, you change your life. You realize how powerful you can be and how many wonderful things there are in this world, despite all of the tragedies. Your impact may seem small at first, but you'll realize that even small changes are better than no progress at all. Most importantly, you will understand that you matter to other people and that you are needed because you are fulfilling an important purpose. Your life is certainly worth living and the world is worth changing.

PART III

CHANGING
YOUR WORLD

"It's time for greatness—not for greed. It's a time for idealism—not ideology. It is a time not just for compassionate words, but compassionate action."
— Marian Wright Edelman

Now that you've developed your Global Purpose and seen how important it can be to your life, it's time to put it into action and change your world. There are infinite ways you can live out your Global Purpose. This section provides examples of different opportunities to make a meaningful difference. Choose the best option for your issue, your life goals, and the lifestyle you wish to have. You can combine several different approaches, creating a website and going on a service vacation, for example. Or you can focus on one. Throughout this section, you can gain inspiration from the examples of people who have made successful efforts to improve the world. Imitate what they have done, or try your own new ideas.

Be sure to visit *www.ChangeTheWorldChangeYourLife.com* and the *Change the World, Change Your Life* Facebook page to connect with other people like yourself who care about improving our world. Through this site, you'll find a community of people doing what they can to make a meaningful difference and live a valuable life. Remember, we're all in this together. You can share stories about service experiences, both good and bad. You can also receive encouragement on how to keep going when times get difficult from people who really understand, and you can support others in their efforts to change the world. Post your middle-of-the-night ideas and get honest feedback from others.

In addition, you can share what's working and what isn't with others. By doing this, other people who care about a Sphere of Service similar to yours can learn from your mistakes and you can learn from theirs. The website is essentially a testing ground and global laboratory for trying new, innovative approaches to the challenges that have plagued our globe for years.

There are also lots of resources on the site that have successfully helped people like you raise money, meet with political leaders, get their causes into newspapers and on TV, and recruit volunteers. These guides provide easy-to-follow advice that can help you be as effective as possible.

CHAPTER 9

Virtual Visionary

"Find a way to get in the way."
—CONGRESSMAN JOHN LEWIS

You can never underestimate the power of the Internet to make your Global Purpose happen. There are numerous ways you can go online and make a meaningful difference. Starting an organization isn't necessary, and this is something you can do on your own or with a team.

Online service is particularly suited for those who are already skilled in using the Internet. However, just because you may not have started the next eBay, hacked into Bank of America, or created a website doesn't mean that you can't use this option. The potential impact you can have on solving community problems is enormous. It is inexpensive and the schedule commitment is completely up to you. Getting started is time intensive, but it requires little time to maintain once you have set up your online platform. For example, building a website to educate college students about the dangers of drunk driving may take a few weekends each month to get an attractive, effective website. Afterwards, though, it's really just a matter of adding content to your site whenever you want. It's all up to you.

ONLINE ADVANTAGES

Here are some ways you can create an online presence to live your Global Purpose.

Getting Attention

If you want to create awareness about a certain social problem or form a way for people to communicate about a community issue, online action is one of the best options you've got. This is especially true if you have striking and possibly controversial pictures that relate to your vision. They should stick in the minds of anyone who views your site. If you want to generate attention about orphaned children in Africa, having pictures of overflowing orphanages on your website could really be effective. The options for getting attention for your issue are limitless.

Communicating

Your vision might be focused on helping people communicate. For example, you might want to start a website that provides people in your town a way to discuss a controversial community issue. If the union of a huge corporation is on strike, and it seems that neither side is communicating effectively, you could make a website showing both sides of the issue. This may bring a greater sense of understanding to the parties involved and help them reach a mutually agreeable compromise. Your website would act, in effect, as a mediator between the two groups.

Organizing

The Internet can help you to organize people. You do not have to simply issue an urgent cry to action. You can use a blog, website, or other resource to actually bring people together. If your vision is to form a way for mothers of disabled children to share insights into their common situation, a website might be a helpful way to do this. It doesn't have to be restricted to your neighborhood. You can use inexpensive webcams or Skype (free!) to have virtual visits with people across the world.

Educating

If your vision is to inform people about a world issue, the Internet is one of the best ways of doing so. You can put tons of detailed information on a website. For example, if you were diagnosed with a rare disease when you were a teenager, your vision might be to help other teens who have just been diagnosed with the disease understand what it is like to go through treatments and live with the symptoms. A blog narrating your experiences can be a valuable resource to anyone who is going through the same situation. They can read about your experiences and know what to expect and how to work with their doctors effectively.

Web Consulting

If you are gifted with website design or simply enjoy making things happen online, one thing you might consider doing after you complete your vision is help other people accomplish their Global Purposes. You now have an incredibly valuable skill set. This would not necessarily be a significant demand on your time. Most people just need to learn the basics of how to create and update a website.

Even if you don't know how to build websites, if you're good with computers you can volunteer online. You can do research, translate information, write, edit, or manage projects from a selection of nonprofit organizations related to your Sphere of Service. This is a great way to get involved even if you have difficulty making solid time commitments each week. For more information about how to do this, visit *www.onlinevolunteering.org*.

◼

Lisa Spodak
"I feel like I'm doing something important. I've
gotten a lot of my friends involved and we have
a lot of fun. I'm proud that I reach a lot of people."

Over just a few years' time, Lisa's mother, stepmother, and cousin were all diagnosed with breast cancer. In the past, Lisa had done short-distance 5K walks for causes including HIV/AIDS and Alzheimer's, but this time she wanted to focus her efforts on breast cancer. She also wanted to do something that would make a bigger impact, so she decided to personally challenge herself by participating in the 2002 Avon Walk for Breast Cancer. In order to participate, Lisa would have to begin intense physical training so that she would have the stamina necessary to finish. The Walk covered more than thirty-nine miles (one and a half marathons!). In addition, all participants in the Avon Walks are required to raise at least $1,800 to benefit breast cancer research and treatment. These seemed like significant challenges.

To accomplish this, Lisa began sending out emails to friends, family members, and other people she knew, asking for donations. Her efforts were successful, and she was able to raise about $4,400, more than twice the amount she needed. She also began training in May so that she would have the endurance necessary for the October event.

By the time of the Walk, Lisa was ready to complete the entire distance. However, rain started pouring on the second day of the event and the remainder of the Walk had to be cancelled. Disappointed that she would not get to finish, Lisa decided to walk again the next year.

This time, she was able to raise $7,800. Being able to complete the walk was a very fulfilling experience. Lisa also gained confidence in her ability to fundraise and contribute to a worthwhile cause.

Eventually, she decided to expand her fundraising efforts and aspired to walk in each of the eight Avon Walks held across the country that year. To accomplish this, Lisa realized that getting donations from people outside her personal contacts would be imperative.

She came up with the idea of holding auctions to raise money. Lisa lived in New York City and was a fan of Broadway shows, so she began bringing Avon breast cancer teddy bears with her to stage doors. Her goal was to get actors, actresses, and other famous people to sign them before and after shows. Lisa's first successful bear-signing was with actor Hugh Jackman, who was starring in *Boy from Oz* at the time. Thrilled that her idea worked, she recruited a team of friends to help.

Now Lisa admits to keeping a bear with her at all times, just in case she happens to see someone famous. Her efforts have been amazingly successful, and she has been able to get entertainers including Matt Damon, Kim Cattrall, Ellen DeGeneres, Jay Leno, Jimmy Kimmel, Pierce Brosnan, and Donny Osmond to sign bears for breast cancer auctions. She has also begun selling t-shirts, calendars, boxing gloves, Mother's Day cards, and other items online at *CafePress.com* and through her website, *LisaWalks.com*. The shirts display catchy phrases such as "Save the Boobs" and "Squish a Boob, Save a Life." In total, Lisa has participated in fifteen Avon Walks and raised more than $110,000 to help find a cure for breast cancer.

Being a part of the walks has been a way for Lisa to do something meaningful to help people like her mother and other relatives suffering from breast cancer. It has also been fun. The walks give Lisa something important to focus on, and she's met some really great people. Getting bears signed, selling shirts, planning the auctions, and completing the walks takes significant time and effort, but working with friends makes it enjoyable. She has also been able to structure exercise into her schedule as she prepares for the long-distance events.

Lisa was recently invited by Avon to attend the opening ceremony of a new breast cancer center. This was a very rewarding experience because she felt like her efforts had been worthwhile. She had helped contribute to something really important.

■

GETTING STARTED WITH A WEBSITE

Write Up

The first thing you need to do is write or type up everything you want to put on your website. This is the written content that you will be displaying to enact your Global Purpose. The content will depend on what you're trying to do. If you are making an educational website to explain the atrocities of prostitution in your local community, it would be a good idea to describe the problem using all the knowledge you've gained. The thirty-second *who, what, when, where,* and *why* are what you want to highlight here.

If you are making a site to get people's attention, the same thing applies. You need to tell them what concerns you before you ask them to do something about it. It's generally a good idea to be sharp and to-the-point with your wording. Think about the people who will be visiting your website. Do you want them to spend a long time on your site? Do you think they are likely to do so if you put a lot of content on there? Shorter is generally better. People want to get the basic facts, and they want to get them fast. Put your most important information at the top so that people who visit your site will be more likely to take a look at what you want them to learn. The same thing holds true for any type of website that you create.

Look at Other Sites

Before building a website, try going online and looking at the sites you like to visit. What makes them stand out? Is it the content that draws you in, or is it something else? Looking at websites for big nonprofits can be helpful here as well. How do they present their information? Depending on the subject matter, some of it may be research-intensive, providing detailed information about the latest academic studies about a social issue. Others may be more focused on the social and emotional effects of a global problem.

Be sure to visit sites that are addressing social issues that are similar to your vision. Get ideas for how you can fill the gaps in what's already out there. What can make your website interesting and unique? If you have trouble coming up with ideas, try making your website personal. People are generally most interested in learning about other people—what makes them spark, what gets them going.

Tell your story. Think about all of the YouTube videos that have gone viral and been viewed by millions upon millions of people. Many of them are created by some bored person with a cheap video camera. However, they all have one thing that sets them apart—they are uniquely personal. You would be smart to do this with your website as well. Why does living your Global Purpose matter to you?

Name Your Site

Naming your site can be both exciting and cause lots of frustration. The best way to do this is to think about your vision. What is your Sphere of Service? Try to pick a site name that reflects the issue area that you are addressing. I did not choose "www. angelaperkey.com" for the Students Serve site for several reasons. First of all, it had nothing to do with the organization I had started and the focus area that I had chose. Who would go to a website named for a person in order to get an academic service grant?

Come up with several phrases that contain a maximum of three or four words each to describe what you are trying to do. Think about other words that describe what you are doing. You want to be as descriptive as possible in as few words as possible. Did you narrow your focus down to a specific neighborhood? You want people to know what you're about just by looking at the name. Again, it may be helpful to think of other websites and the names they use.

Your web address does not have to be the same as you website's name, but it could be helpful in getting other people to visit your website. Remember that your name needs to be different from anyone else's. If you find that someone else has created a similar site to focus on problems in their neighborhood, you can adopt their title by making it specific to your target area.

Once you have a list of potential names, go online and see if these names are available. Here are a couple of sites where you can check to see if your site name is open: Network Solutions (*www.networksolutions.com*) or Register (*www.register.com*).

Chances are, many of your potential website names will be already taken. If this is the case, there are still plenty of options. Play around by adding the name of your city or something else that can distinguish your site. For example, you wanted to name your website "diabetes.com" but found that this was already taken. So instead, you search for "diabetesindallas.com" and find that this is available. There are plenty of available names out there. Be creative. Ask others for help if you want feedback and suggestions.

Don't forget to watch your spelling. You don't want to build a website called "www.philanthropyinphonix.com" when what you really wanted was "www.philanthropyin*phoenix*.com." This is an unfortunate example of how to prevent people from finding your site.

Find a Provider

Once you have a name for your site, you need to pick the service provider. The service provider is also referred to as the hosting site. By paying a certain amount of money to the service provider, you will be able to keep your website online for a specific amount of time. Usually, the service providers offer discounts on longer-term purchases. You can make the best decision for what fits your budget and the purposes of your vision. Think of this as paying rent.

The following websites have inexpensive hosting options available:

- Blue Host
  www.bluehost.com
  (I have been really pleased with Blue Host. Their customer support hotline is outstanding.)
- Web Hosting Pad
  www.webhostingpad.com
- Go Daddy
  www.godaddy.com

It's a good idea to go with a reputable service provider. The quality of free website design templates and tools varies significantly. It is really important to investigate this before purchasing hosting services for a year or more. You could always switch hosts later, even if your "lease" was not up yet, but this can be a pain and is something else you'll have to deal with. It's best to go first class here.

Website Design

You will find that your hosting server probably offers a selection of formatting templates and tools that you can use to build your website. Read the information or help section on your hosting server to learn more about how to use them. If you have questions, you can always call their help lines. Some servers have instant messaging help desks as well, which offer immediate gratification.

You can also buy software that enables you to make a website without learning html. These programs are relatively cheap and not exceedingly complicated. I really enjoyed playing around

CHANGE THE WORLD, CHANGE YOUR LIFE

with one of these, WebEasy7, when I got it free after buying tax preparation software.

Another option is to ask or pay someone to do this for you. It is likely that someone you know has already learned how to design a website. Get them to work with you. High-school and college students are good resources. They may be younger than you are, but they probably know what they are talking about. There are also freelance web designers who work for hourly rates. Depending on how complex your site is, you should probably be able to hire someone for a reasonable rate. If you explain what your vision is, they might even give you a discount. You can look up web developers in the Yellow Pages or check out these sites that have lists of web builders for temporary projects: Elance (*www.elance.com*) or Craigslist (*www.craigslist.com*).

Patience

It is inevitable that you are going to hit some snags in building your website. Be prepared for this and definitely don't let it stop you. Doing anything for the first time is difficult, but you will learn once you become familiar with the different processes. For example, maintaining the site is much simpler than building it. Depending on the complexity of the website, it is likely that you can make all of the necessary updates even if you hired someone else to build it for you.

One more thing you will want to remember is to be creative. Crazy fonts and Arabic may appear on your site out of nowhere, but go with this. Find a way to work around it if you cannot fix it. Unfortunately, I've had experiences with this on the Students Serve site where entire sections of our website have gone missing for certain periods of time for no apparent reason. The great thing here is that you learn to be flexible.

Updates

Once you build your site and are pleased with the basic layout and content, you need to make sure that you don't leave it at that. Update it with new information as frequently as possible. The number of times you post new information will vary depending on the purpose of your site. For example, awareness, communication, and organizing sites should be updated relatively often. Education sites are less likely to need refreshed information unless new research comes out. When people come back to your site and see that things have changed, they will continue to visit on a more regular basis.

Connections with Other Sites

Try to find other people who have websites for similar interests as your site. See if you can contact the owner of the site and work out a deal in which you link to each other's sites. People who visit your website might find someone else's point of view, information, or services to be helpful as well. The same is true when someone visits the other person's site. By putting links to other people's sites, both website owners benefit. The viewers do, too. They are able to find even more information than one site alone provides.

Traffic

Once your website has been launched, you will likely want was many people as possible to visit. Building traffic to your site is pretty challenging. I've talked with some experienced professionals about this, and they've advised me to get as big a net presence as possible. What they mean by this is to not only have my website, but also to be active online in other ways that can give the site attention. Writing in other people's blogs and including your website address is recommended. This is especially true if the blogs are related to the topic of your website. Posting YouTube videos is another way of driving traffic to your site.

I recommend that you tell everyone you know about your website and encourage them to visit it. If you are ever interviewed for a newspaper story or TV show, be sure to mention your website and ask the reporter to include it in the write-up. You might be surprised at how many people become interested and go to your site.

Also, make sure that you add a signature tagline in all of your emails that has your website address on it. Every time someone reads an email from you, he will see the link. When you launch your new website, sending a website "birthday announcement" to everyone in your email address book is another option. Ask them to forward the message on to everyone they know, especially those they think would benefit from the site or be interested in visiting it.

BLOGGING

One of the cheapest and easiest ways to make your vision happen online is to start a blog. Blogging is a good way to tell other people about your experiences. It generates attention and awareness of the world problems that you think are important. It's probably best to keep your blog focused on your Global Purpose and not multiple issues.

Starting a blog is much less complicated than starting and building a website. There are lots of good, free blog hosts. They will likely put ads on your blog, but your content should still be front and center. And it's absolutely free. Plus, unlike a website, you don't have to build the technical structure behind a blog. All you have to do is pour yourself and your vision into the blog so that your personality comes through.

It's important to note that the blog does not have to be about your personal experiences or musings on life. You can use it to enable others to voice their opinion. For example, suppose you have a vision to educate people in Philadelphia about what it is like to be homeless. Instead of writing the blog yourself, you could visit local homeless people and ask them to tell you about their experiences. Instead of theorizing about the problem or relying on obscure research papers, you would be enabling the homeless to share their point of view. I would certainly be interested in reading a blog like this.

Any of these sites should work. All you have to do is sign up. You get to choose the colors, fonts, backgrounds, and all of the fun stuff. Customize it with your name and the other basic details about yourself and what you want the blog to be. Within a few minutes, you can start writing.

Here are some free blog sites:

- WordPress
  www.wordpress.com
- Blogger
  www.blogger.com
- Xanga
  www.xanga.com
- Live Journal
  www.livejournal.com

YOUTUBE

Finally, you can make a video that highlights your Global Purpose. The purpose of your video can be to show the world your focus issue. Few things are more effective than actually seeing the real thing: the decrepit living conditions of individuals in poor Indian villages, a homeless man talking about his experience. This is a great way to educate other people and get them to care about what your vision is.

Making a video is simple, and all you need is a home video camera. Design a script or frame-by-frame format of what you want to go into your video. It could be as simple as you talking to the camera about your vision. Another possibility is to interview other people.

In researching your vision about reducing high rates of obesity in low-income people in Nashville, you might learn that many people do not have access to grocery stores within five miles of their house. They have to eat at nearby fast-food restaurants because they do not have cars and bringing groceries back on the bus is difficult. They do not have the money to pay for a taxi. Find these people and go talk to them. Ask them if you can film what they have to say. This is much more compelling than just writing about the facts.

CHAPTER 10

Finding Funds

"Lack of money is no obstacle.
Lack of an idea is an obstacle."
— KEN HAKUTA

Whatever your Global Purpose is, you are probably going to need at least a small number of funds to get started. Most people are surprised to know that it takes money to form a nonprofit organization. I certainly was. Before I started Students Serve, I didn't realize that I would have to come up with a little over $400 just to become an official organization and to get tax-exempt status from the IRS. This was before we ever gave out any grants.

Don't worry about the money, though. There are numerous ways to get funds. In the coming pages, you will learn how to find the money you need to accomplish your vision. Many people give donations to receive a deduction in their income taxes. You can direct your own personal giving toward your Global Purpose, and you'll discover how to raise money and convince others to financially support your service.

FIND A FIGURE

The first thing you need to do is estimate how much accomplishing your vision is going to cost. This is not an exact science, and it may be difficult to forecast how much money you will need. If you are forming a nonprofit organization, you will need to pay for the official government filing fees. You will likely need stamps, envelopes, and paper if you're going to write letters to generate awareness about the importance of contacting members of Congress about the high costs of health insurance. A website is typically not free. Go online and figure out how much a domain name and site hosting for a year will cost. If you are going on a service vacation or a mission trip, you need to estimate how much it will cost to travel, eat, stay overnight, and enact your service plans.

Try not to go overboard with the expenses, and remember what your goal is. It's to change your world and your life. You may already have many of the things you'll need, so ordering stationery with the name of your nonprofit or cause emblazoned on it in glossy letters isn't necessary. You probably have plenty of pens and paper, and your own printer and ink should be fine for printing fundraising letters. If you're heading to the Dominican Republic on a service trip, book a comfortable, safe, and reasonably priced hotel room. To reduce the cost even further, you could probably even find a family who would be willing to host you at their home for a modest fee. A side benefit is that you would get to know them and see how people really live there.

■

FINDING FUNDS

Cosmo and Shin Fujiyama

"I'll be a part of this as long as I'm alive. I've seen with my
own eyes that people's lives have been transformed."

Cosmo was passionate about improving women's rights in Latin
America. In the past, she had made several extended trips to Peru
and Nicaragua to teach English and increase awareness about
women's equality. However, it was a trip to Honduras in the summer of 2005 that changed her life.

Cosmo and her older brother, Shin, were in the country at the
same time. As they walked the streets of El Progreso, the fourth
largest city in Honduras, they met hundreds of children, most of
whom lived in lean-to shelters constructed of plastic and metal
sheeting. The children could not afford to go to the doctor or to
attend secondary school. Many families were even too poor to buy
land on which to live. They simply couldn't afford these luxuries.
Cosmo and Shin were shocked and emotionally moved by the experience.

After returning home, Shin and Cosmo started asking people
they knew to help promote change in the community of El Progreso. They focused their efforts on the families of the area's largest
squatter community, Siete de Abril, and the children of the over-
crowded Copprome Orphanage.

At first, Cosmo and Shin collected coins and used the money
to send pens and pencils to the children in the orphanage. Then
they sold Christmas cards to raise money for El Progreso. With the
money they earned, they were able to pay for school tuition and
uniforms for the poorest students in the community. Eventually,
in February 2006, they formed a nonprofit organization, Students

Helping Honduras. Since that time, Cosmo has spent nearly two years in El Progreso, and Shin has been living there half of that time. He spends the rest of the year raising money in the United States to fund their service.

Through Students Helping Honduras, Cosmo and Shin have been able to raise hundreds of thousands of dollars and have built an education center at the orphanage. In 2007, they were able to construct homes for seventy-two families in Siete de Abril, as well as a temporary school building. They are currently in the process of constructing forty-five new houses. In the future, they plan to build a children's home and recruit several long-term volunteers.

Cosmo and Shin have developed a newfound love and appreciation for each other. Growing up, they were so involved with their own activities that they rarely saw each other. Now, they are closer than ever before. Living in Honduras, they share a bedroom, a car, an office, and jobs. They rarely spend time apart from each other. Cosmo says that she doesn't trust anyone like she trusts her brother.

Cosmo believes that she has really grown as a person since going to Honduras. Being in Honduras amidst the stark poverty has been emotionally challenging. Yet she has developed an emotional maturity and a mental toughness that she never possessed before. She has also learned to be patient. There is not an instant solution to the seemingly endless problems, and this can be frustrating. Yet Cosmo and Shin would never trade this life experience. Since first coming to Honduras, Cosmo has seen the lives of others transform. This includes her own life. She sees the world in a new light.

■

RAISING FUNDS

Fundraising is the most common way to get the money you need to change the world. It's important to keep in mind that you will probably be most effective if you develop a creative new way to fundraise. In addition, when you begin, it's best not to "beg" for money, especially from people you don't know. This is generally not an effective way to get donations because people typically don't want to give to strangers. Ask the people you know first. Here are some techniques I have found to be helpful and that other people have used successfully.

Get the Three Fs—Friends, Fools, and Family—Involved

Tell them what you want to do and why. Explain your plan and show them how much money you need to make it happen. Let them know how much it will mean to you once this is accomplished. Invite them to help in other ways as well, and make them part of your team. They have more to offer than just their money.

Host a Tea Party

Or a tailgating party, brunch, lunch, or any other social food event. Invite people over from your work, church, sports team, or anywhere else. Tell them about your ideas and get them on board. Be sure to ask the friends of your friends for support. You might not be comfortable asking for financial help at this time, but be sure to mention what you will need to make this a success. Ask if they have any ideas. Later, be sure to send letters thanking them for dropping by and asking for a contribution of either their money or time. If they can't do either of these, ask if they know anyone who could.

Have a "Non-event"

To have a non-event, send out invitations to people you know saying that you are hosting a fundraiser. However, instead of asking them to come to another event, you are asking them to contribute money. This way, all of the money goes toward your cause and not a big dinner. Be sure to send a personal letter explaining what your Global Purpose is and why it's important to you. They will be much more likely to give.

Ask Your Boss

I was able to get the firm where I work to become a corporate sponsor of Students Serve. Many employers will be excited that you are taking the initiative to do something as important as this. They will likely want to help you out. They may ask for name recognition for their contributions, but that is easy to give them in exchange for their support. Don't be shy about asking! They might even be willing to start a company-wide effort to support your work.

Partner with Sue and Mike's Hot Chicken

One year, we had a Students Serve night at a locally owned Mexican restaurant. The restaurant made us a deal in which we would get 15 percent of the profits made from everyone who ordered from their restaurant on Friday night and said they were with Students Serve. The staffers and I posted fliers all over campus advertising the date and restaurant. The restaurant benefited from our free advertising. We made some money and didn't even have to host an event. It was great—a win-win situation. This is just one way to collaborate with businesses; the options are endless. The best way to go about doing this is to think about how you can benefit the business as well as your Global Purpose.

Use the Internet

Through Facebook campaigns, ad revenue on your website or blog, eBay auctions, donation buttons on your site, and many other ways, you can raise money to make your vision a reality. This doesn't have to be limited to raising money, though. You could also ask that people send you used books or clothing.

You will need to describe who you are and why people should send you money, books, shoes, or whatever it is you are trying to collect. Be sure that you are very specific about where the money is going and why you are the best person to use it. You are really trying to sell yourself and your vision here. Explaining the positive effects donating will have on the community and the world will also help you be as effective as possible.

By using websites to meet people who have similar Global Purposes, you can coordinate your efforts to have an even bigger impact on solving the issues that you care about. For example, if you're raising money to fund mental health clinics, you can partner with several people across the country or around the globe who are also concerned about this issue. Instead of just doing a walkathon or fundraiser in your hometown and taking on the challenge of coordinating everything by yourself, you can team up and help each other out.

FUNDRAISING LETTERS

Sending fundraising letters to people you know is another method for funding your service efforts. The most effective letters explain what you are doing, why you are doing it, and how others can support you.

You can take a look at my first fundraising letters online at *www.ChangeTheWorldChangeYourLife.com.* There are also templates for event invitations that you can use.

Saving Stamps

Instead of mailing fundraising letters to potential donors or sending newsletters to give updates to your supporters, you may want to consider using emails and e-newsletters instead. You can still stay connected with people who care about your Global Purpose, but this saves a lot of money. It can also be easier to manage the contact information of a large number of people.

Although there are many options for doing this, one business that you may want to look into is called Emma (named after an abbreviated version of email marketing). Located online at *www.myemma.com,* the web-based company helps you manage all of your email and marketing efforts for your Global Purpose. The pricing is reasonable and nonprofit organizations can get a 20 percent discount off everything if they sign up for a year's worth of services. Plus, Emma plants five trees for every new customer that joins them. The business also gives its services away for free to twenty-five nonprofits each year.

FIND A GRANT OR FELLOWSHIP

You might be able to find funding for your efforts through a foundation, the government, or nonprofit organization. In all honesty, filling out grant applications can be a pain. However, it can be well worth your effort. Apply only for the ones that you think are well suited to your Global Purpose. Explain who you are, why you want to do this, the skills you have that make this a good fit, and how you plan to do it. Why should they give you money? Be as personable and honest as possible. Make sure that you do not play down your credentials in an effort to be modest. Instead, sell yourself. That is basically what every grant application asks for.

If you need help finding opportunities that are a good match for you and your project, go online and do a search. Be prepared to spend some time doing this and try not to get frustrated. Before you start applying for grants, keep in mind that this can be quite an undertaking. Here are some places to start:

- The Foundation Center
  www.foundationcenter.org/getstarted/individual
- Government grants—(these typically go to big organizations, but you might give it a shot)
  www.grants.gov
- Idealist
  www.idealist.org/en/career/fellowship.html
- The Community Foundation
  See if there is one close to where you live. Search "The Community Foundation [your city here]" to find the organization closest to your home.
- Center for Nonprofit Management
  Like the Community Foundation, see if there is a Center for Nonprofit Management in your area.
- Students Serve (I couldn't resist!)
  www.studentsserve.org

CORPORATE SPONSORSHIPS

You can get money for your efforts by getting corporations to sponsor your nonprofit organization or events. These endorsements can be great for both your cause and the business that sponsors you. I like to refer to them as MBPs, mutually beneficial partnerships.

First, think of businesses (preferably local businesses) that could benefit from being associated with your organization. For example, if you're working to provide healthy after-school snacks to low-income kids, you could ask a restaurant to support your efforts.

Next, come up with benefits that you could offer them. This could be putting their logo on your website as a "Corporate Sponsor" or hanging a banner for the company at one of your fundraising events. You could let the owner or another company leader speak at your event and then present them with a plaque that they can display at their offices.

Define ways that the corporations can help your business. It's important to remember that not all donations have to be money. Restaurants can donate food; bookstores can donate books; accounting firms can offer their workers for an afternoon of volunteering.

With Students Serve, I was able to get my employer to become a corporate sponsor of the organization. The "Big Four" accounting firm I worked for was trying to recruit college students to apply for jobs, and sponsoring Students Serve helped them present a positive image. In exchange for a monetary donation, we agreed to place the company logo on our website and do what we could to assist them with good publicity.

This is a large company, and it has a community relations employee whose job includes coordinating employees for volunteer opportunities. I spoke with her about Students Serve and explained the purpose of the organization. She became enthusiastic about what I was trying to do and encouraged me to apply for a donation from the company. I submitted a two-page description of the organization and described how we could create an MBP. A few weeks later, I was notified that the executive committee in charge of dispersing funds had agreed to become our first corporate sponsor.

SELL YOUR SERVICES

I'm not implying anything immoral here, but you can raise a lot of money by offering your services to others. You might feel as if you're six years old again, but have fun with this. Wash other people's cars, clean their bathrooms, post their old furniture on Craigslist, feed their cats when they go on vacation.

I know that offering your services may seem like a last resort for most people, but it is certainly an honorable and effective way to get the money you need. I know of a group of college students who offered to clean other student's dorm bathrooms in exchange for a donation to help pay the costs of a trip to build houses in impoverished Latin American communities. They worked hard doing this and made a decent amount of money. The only thing it cost was their sweat, soap, and maybe a bit of their egos.

Tell your temporary employer why you're working and charge a premium for your services. They will pay more because they know that you are raising money to serve others. And even if you don't leave their bathroom faucet sparkling, they will be much more likely to take pity.

SELL STUFF

A more palatable alternative to selling your sweat is to sell things. Every year, you see the Girl Scouts out in front of the grocery stores getting people to buy their delicious Thin Mints and Tag-alongs. They make tons of money this way. Adopt their idea and ask local stores if you can sell something outside the entrance. It really helps if you are benefiting a local cause or working with a nonprofit organization. Bring out your inner Edison, Ford, or da Vinci! You can also create products to get the money you need. More resources on how to do this are available online.

If you're good at baking cookies or making arts and crafts, you might want to plan a bake sale or craft sale. These work especially well at events, and you would probably be surprised at how much money you could make. Combine the sale with a concert, parent-teacher night, or some other event that people are coming to anyway. Also, be sure to ask your event host for permission prior to selling your goods. You might need to offer them a cut of the proceeds to get an okay, but if you're success-ful, it'll be worth it.

A huge yard sale is another good option. Get your neighbors, friends, and anyone you know to donate their old things. You can also do this on eBay or Craigslist. See if your newspaper will run a free ad in the classifieds and tell everyone you know about the sale. In addition, be sure that you remember to have a jar for donations and a flyer that you can show people. If your prices are still reasonable but a little on the high side, people will pay when they know what you're working for. They might even make an additional donation.

These are the most common ideas for raising money by sell-ing things, but don't limit yourself to these options. Be creative. Get back in touch with your inner Girl/Boy Scout.

Citrus Sales and Singing

Fundraising can be made into a type of game. Selling things to other people can be a lot of fun, and you may be surprised with how much money you can raise for your cause. When I was in middle school I participated in the Nashville Children's Choir. There were three different choirs that made up the Nashville Children's Choir—the Preparatory Choir for beginners, a middle level choir, and the more advanced Touring Choir. One of the benefits of being in the Touring Choir was that you got to go on a week-long trip with the group to sing in other places. It was an honor to be in this group, which had performed at Carnegie Hall, and the annual trip was the highlight of the year.

In my first year in the Touring Choir, we were scheduled to go to Boston. I was so excited and couldn't wait for the end of the year. However, my parents said that I would have to raise half of the money in order to be able to go on the trip. This seemed daunting at first, but the choir sponsored a citrus fruit fundraiser to help members pay for part of the cost of the trip.

In the fall, we were given order forms that displayed boxes of Indian River red grapefruit and juicy navel oranges. We were told to sell as much as we could and that half of the proceeds would be gathered into an account to offset the costs of the Boston trip. Each week during the fundraiser, there were also prizes such as Beanie Babies and candy that we could choose from if we sold above a certain amount of fruit.

For me, the race was on once I was given the order form. My dad went with me, and I knocked on doors across the neighborhood. Every night after school and during the weekends, I would ring the doorbells and deliver my sales pitch, explaining the choir and Boston trip. My parents put up order forms at their offices, and the grocery store was generous and let me set up a table on weekends to sell the fruit.

In the end, I sold over $800 worth of fruit and was able to go to Boston, which was exciting. Because of all the work I had done, I really enjoyed the trip and appreciated the opportunity. In the process, I even amassed a significant Beanie Baby collection and gained valuable insights into fundraising and selling to other people.

FEAR AND FUNDRAISING

I was a bit timid about fundraising at first. To be honest, I didn't even tell my parents that I had started Students Serve until I had filed the papers to become an official nonprofit organization. They were certainly surprised. But they were also overwhelmingly supportive, and this really made the difference for me. They believed in my abilities and knew that starting the nonprofit was something I cared about. I used our family Christmas letter list to get additional donations. The support of family and friends was invaluable, and I wish I had told everyone earlier.

Remember that your Global Purpose is important to you. If you doubt yourself or how important your vision is, pull out those pages you printed about the problem you are solving. The need is huge, and if you are not willing to do it, then who will? Dive right in. Call your sister, brother, or best friend. If they truly love and care for you, they will be excited right along with you. They may not be able to give you their money, but they *can* give you their encouragement. This means more than anything.

You really have nothing to loose. Make that call. Send out that invitation. You will surely never regret it.

<h2 align="center">LEARNING FROM
FUNDRAISING FAILURES</h2>

As much as I would like to say that all of our Students Serve fundraisers were resounding successes, that would simply not be true. We have had our share or fundraising flops and will likely continue to do so in the future.

One of my "brilliant ideas" for fundraising was to send out letters to recent alumni of William and Mary. In the letter, we explained what we were doing and who we were and then asked for a contribution to our efforts. We even sent out the letters with self-addressed stamped envelopes inside, making them more than twice as expensive as just mailing the letter. Weeks went by as we anticipated dozens of our letters returning to Students Serve with checks for student grants tucked inside. Nothing came. After about a month of waiting, I gave up hope. No one sent us a donation. Sad!

This happens, though. It's not a bad reflection on you. It just means you need to pursue a different strategy. One way to help with this is to do test runs when sending out fundraising letters. Instead of sending your letter to five hundred people, start with just twenty-five. If you get positive responses you can then send out the letter to more people with greater confidence that your efforts will be successful.

I remember one year in Nashville when I was about twelve years old. There was an intense mayoral campaign race going on, and my dad was familiar with one of the candidates and his wife. In an effort to help with the campaign, our family hosted a reception at our house in honor of our favored candidate. We invited all of our friends and acquaintances, and it was scheduled for a Sunday afternoon at 2:00 p.m. My mom had cooked some fabulous treats for the event, and the house was spotless. The candidate and his family were there a few minutes early, so we were just waiting for our guests. Two o'clock came and went with no guests showing up. We waited and waited and ate and waited. Two-thirty came and went. Still no guests. By the end of the reception, only one person had bothered to show up. It was our rental house occupant who was dropping by to pay her rent. At least she stayed to meet the candidate and eat some brownies.

Whenever something like this happens, the best thing to do is to try to laugh it off. Don't panic. In the end, things worked out well. Our family got to spend the afternoon with the future mayor of Nashville and his family. At one point, I even played the trumpet for our guests. They were very gracious.

> "Be who you are and say what you feel, because those who mind don't matter and those who matter don't mind."
> —Dr. Seuss

THANK-YOU NOTES

Sending thank-you notes makes all the difference when fundraising. Your mother probably made you do this when you were younger, and she really did know what she was saying. You want the people who have given you assistance to know how much they mean to you and how much you appreciate them. This is not only polite, it's smart. They will be much more likely to give funds again if you thank them and tell them exactly how you are using their money. A phone call might be nice, as well. Share the love and thank your supporters.

■

Amy Kapczynski

According to Universities Allied for Essential Medicines (UAEM), ten million people die each year from diseases that have available cures. Furthermore, numerous diseases affecting millions of the world's poorest individuals are overlooked by researchers and drug development companies. Sleeping sickness, blinding trachoma, and lymphatic filariasis are among the "neglected diseases" that affect innumerable impoverished individuals because they do not constitute a sufficient market opportunity to attract commercial drug research and development.

As a twenty-six-year-old law student in 2001, Amy Kapczynski thought that this was inexcusable. She had worked in an AIDS organization in London in the past, and the destruction of these types of diseases was overwhelming. Through further research, she came to realize that major research universities play a critical role in increasing access to medicines and medical research.

Amy and Samantha Chaifetz, who was also in law school at the time, formed a group of students concerned about this issue. Together, they worked with the drug researcher who discovered a critical HIV drug called stavudine (d4T) and successfully pressured Yale University and a major pharmaceutical company into not enforcing the drug's patent in South Africa. This was a landmark event. As a result, the price of the drug fell by more than 95 percent. Since this occurred, the prices of numerous other drugs for neglected diseases declined, as well. Because of their efforts, it is now possible for nongovernmental organizations and governments to provide treatment to HIV patients in low-income countries.

UAEM, a nonprofit organization, was formed following this event to build upon this successful effort and make other drugs accessible at low costs in other developing nations. Colleges and universities own the patent rights to important pharmaceutical drugs that are used to treat HIV/AIDS, cancer, hepatitis B, and countless other diseases. A 2000 United States Senate report stated that fifteen of the twenty-one drugs with the greatest therapeutic impact were developed using research, most of which occurs at universities, funded by American taxpayers. However, many drugs that are developed at universities have remained largely out of reach for millions of impoverished sick individuals around the world.

Now, UAEM has chapters at major research colleges and universities across the globe. Each chapter works to increase access to the drug research and patents that are located within their schools yet inaccessible for producing useful treatments for people in the developing world. Students in medical and law school, as well as undergraduates, lead the efforts of UAEM and initiate projects to support the nonprofit's mission.

The organization has been very successful, and it continues to work on passing new legislation that makes pharmaceutical drugs available in developing nations. The work undertaken by UAEM has been financially supported through private donations and grants from major foundations including the Kaiser Family Foundation, Doris Duke Charitable Foundation, the Ford Foundation, Oxfam America, and the Open Society Institute.

■

CHAPTER 11

It Takes a Team

"Friendship makes prosperity more shining and
lessens adversity by dividing and sharing it."
— CICERO

Although your Global Purpose is your own, unique way of changing the world and improving your life, it is likely that you will
need the help of others. Working with people who care about the
same problems will be a fun and deeply satisfying experience.
The support of other individuals will exponentially increase the
power of your service efforts to make a difference in solving a
community problem. The creativity, knowledge, time, finances,
and man/girlpower of a team of volunteers will be well worth the
time you spend recruiting them to your cause.

At first, you might be reluctant to share your Global Purpose
with others. This is understandable because you have just tied
your personal goals and life plans to making a difference. I felt
this way when I started Students Serve, particularly when I had

to learn how to explain my vision for student grants and how this could improve the world.

However, sharing the service aspects of what you are doing does not require you to divulge your personal ambitions. Simply explain your Sphere of Service, why you chose to focus on this issue, and what you want to do. In time, volunteers will be coming in droves to help, and you will start becoming acclimated to the idea of having others help you accomplish your mission. In the best case scenario, you can find other people who have Global Purposes similar to yours. Just think of the potential you will have when combining forces with others!

BUILDING YOUR CORPS

If you need people to help you on a regular basis with work that does not require specialized skills, contact everyone you know and tell them what you are doing. For example, if you are stuffing, licking, and stamping envelopes in an effort to increase local teacher pay, this is the time when you need as many people as possible to get involved. From experience, I know how much time it can take to send out a lot of letters (and how tired you can get of tasting envelope glue). The more volunteers, the better.

If you don't know enough people, there are several ways to attract them. One of the easiest is to post a flier in your church, workplace, favorite café, or anywhere else you go on a regular basis. Another way to recruit some help is to send out a mass email to friends, family, and everyone you know on Facebook. Have an "envelope party" and invite everybody to come and help. Ask them to forward the email to everyone they know who lives nearby. Be sure to put a line in your email saying that each person who can help will make a valuable contribution to the cause and that your efforts would not be possible without their help. Posting Students Serve volunteer opportunities on Craigslist has been really effective, and I've been able to meet some dedicated volunteers by doing this. Of course, you have to be careful and make sure that the people who respond to your posting genuinely want to help out and don't have another, malicious motive.

Another method to start building your corps of volunteers is to go to an event, such as a concert, flea market, or church picnic that you know will have many people in attendance. Print up small fliers on colorful paper and distribute them. One way I did this for Students Serve was to hand out fliers at the annual campus activities fair at the beginning of the year. I also asked the people who seemed interested for their email addresses and phone numbers. Afterwards, we were able to follow up with the people we knew were interested. (You can find a copy of the flier I distributed at *www.ChangeTheWorldChangeYourLife.com.*)

SUGAR

You can never underestimate the power of brownies and feeding your team of helpers. Betty Crocker, the Pillsbury Doughboy, and Duncan Hines seem to work magic in terms of getting volunteers to work hard and help with everything you need! It even has an effect on getting people to return and help you live your Global Purpose. They will also be more likely to recruit other people to come on board.

Bribery aside, treating your people nicely is really important. Let them know that they matter to you and that they are making your mission possible. Think about how long it would take you to lick that stack of envelopes without the help of your faithful crew. And how bored you would become. They are choosing to spend their time working with you.

The most important thing to keep in mind when working with other people is to make it fun. If they don't enjoy it, they will quit and you probably will as well. In addition, be sure to celebrate. Look at all of the important work that you are doing. You are truly changing your world. If this isn't reason enough for celebration, what is? Don't take yourself too seriously. If you take a moment to appreciate this, it will motivate you to keep going.

GIVING BACK TO YOUR VOLUNTEERS

Volunteers make your Global Purpose happen, and it's important to be able to thank them for their efforts. I've found that the more you can offer to help them, the more likely they will be willing to help you.

With Students Serve, I offered to write recommendation letters for our staff members. We were all applying for jobs, internships, and fellowships, and recommendation letters were required for each of these. As the founder and executive director of Students Serve, I had the ability to write detailed, glowing recommendation letters and provide references for our volunteers. No one had to know that the "Founder and Executive Director" of this organization was another college student. It looked really impressive for our volunteers. I was honest about their exemplary performance and helped several of them get competitive jobs and internships.

EXPERIENCED MINDS

When starting Students Serve, I had no idea how to run an organization. I had some leadership experience, but it was nothing compared to what I would be doing with the nonprofit. Because of this, one of the first things I did was make appointments to meet with some local nonprofit executives. I knew that my organization was infinitely smaller than theirs, but I wanted to get an idea about how they did their jobs, what was important to know, how to find funding, and how to be as effective as possible. Their advice was instructive and really helped me learn how I wanted to establish Students Serve. I took most of what they said and added it into my plans.

At the end of the meetings, I would always ask if they could give me the contact information for someone else who might be able to talk with me. I sent a thank you note the next day and emailed the other people they had referred me to. In these emails, I made sure to mention the person who had told me to speak with them. I got a meeting every time. Eventually, you will have more people to speak with than you need. After several meetings, you will probably find that you have plenty of information to get going on your own.

If you are going to set up a nonprofit, foundation, or start a mission or service trip, it is a great idea to talk to someone else who has done this before and has some experience. Set up a meeting to pick their brains. Learn all you can about the nonprofit community, how to make travel arrangements, or anything else you think will be helpful to know. Ask as many questions as you can. Their advice can be really helpful and keep you from falling into some potential snares.

However, be forewarned that not all of the people you talk with will want to give you advice. Most of the nonprofit leaders I spoke with were encouraging and seemed excited about my efforts to start Students Serve. I am grateful for their kindness and insight into the nonprofit world. Unfortunately, there were a few who essentially told me that there was no need for another nonprofit organization and that my time and efforts would be better spent doing something else.

Please do not let them stop your plans. I realized that many of these discouraging executives felt as though I was competing with them. There is a limited amount of money each year from governments, foundations, and individual donors that is dedicated to funding nonprofit organizations. Even though they did not say it outright, these individuals thought that my organization would siphon funds away from theirs, threatening their ability to accomplish their goals. I represented future competition.

Once you go on your first service trip or start your family foundation or begin to accomplish your vision, you should strive to lift up others who want to do the same thing. Your encouragement will mean more to them than anything else. Tell them the tips and tricks that you have learned along the way. You can let them know the names of people who have been helpful to you and share what you have learned. In addition to changing your world and changing your own life, you will change their lives.

THE ROUNDTABLE

Although they aren't aware of this, I get guidance from former President Jimmy Carter, the character Elle Woods (from the movie *Legally Blonde*), Richard Branson, my grandmother (who passed away in 1996), Truett Cathy (the founder of Chick-fil-A restaurants), Al Gore, and Warren Buffett. We have meetings at least once a month when I get their advice about Students Serve. In one of our latest "meetings," we discussed the best way to expand the organization through the new website, *www.StudentsServe.org*.

I read that having a made-up group of advisors is a great way to think through problems and view potential solutions through the eyes of people you respect. This may seem crazy, but I've tried it and found that it works. Besides, who wouldn't want to get advice from such a talented group of people? My Roundtable counsel consists of people who are living and dead, fictional and real. It is a group of people I respect and want to imitate in some regard. You may want to start your own Roundtable. It does not take much time and is really fun once you get into it. Choose people that you look up to. They don't have to be known for their charitable contributions or efforts to save the world. They can be well-known individuals or your personal heroes. Who knows? You may even get to meet some of these people in person one day.

POLITICIANS AND THE PRESS
(PEOPLE WHO KNOW PEOPLE)

When building a team, you can never underestimate the power of getting help from people who know people. Politicians and individuals in the newspaper business can be some of your strongest allies. They can connect you with numerous people in the local community who can help you make your mission a reality. It is inevitable that whenever undertaking something that requires a lot of money, large donations of goods, or massive awareness, you will likely need to bring in other people for help with publicizing your mission and meeting high-powered people in the community.

Politicians and the press have the connections you need. This takes a lot of effort, but it can pay huge dividends. It is sometimes very difficult to get a meeting with one of these individuals. The key to getting the time you want is persistence. Pick one person you want to meet with and call or email. Like bringing in professional help, you want to tell them who you are, what you are doing, why you are doing it, and ask for a fifteen-minute meeting.

For politicians, it is best to target the individuals who represent your district. This would be your congressman, state senator, state representative, or council member. Depending on the size of your hometown, you might have a difficult time getting a meeting with your mayor. I can say from personal experience that getting a meeting with your governor or one of your senators is incredibly difficult. Start by going for the people with the smallest titles first. Your council member will have lots of connections that can be of great help. Their party affiliation does not matter as long as they have been elected to represent you and your district. It is best to start here when you are just beginning; then you can target higher-powered officials as your experience and credibility improves.

If you get a response after calling or emailing the first time, that's fabulous. You should go into business doing this. In all likelihood, though, you will get no response to your email. If so, call the politician's office and ask the receptionist for the name and email address of the politician's scheduler. Now, email and/ or call this person until you get a meeting. Keep at it. Depending on who you are trying to meet with, this may take weeks or months, so be as flexible with your schedule as possible. Remember that these people are paid by taxpayers to serve you. Remind the scheduler that you are a constituent (and hopefully a voter). Make sure that you are always courteous, kind, and insistent. Never hesitate to call as many times as necessary in order to get the meeting you need.

Once you schedule your meeting, be sure to prepare beforehand because you never want to waste this person's time. Be brief and explain to the politician everything you said in the email. While you have this person's attention, ask for an endorsement. A one-sentence statement that your elected official believes in what your organization is doing can work wonders with fundraising and getting other people to join your efforts. If he or she says no, then so be it. You can remember this on the next Election Day. Yet keep trying to get notable individuals to make positive comments about your service efforts because the potential benefit of an endorsement is enormous.

The process for contacting a reporter is very similar. Find the newspaper reporter who writes about community news. This is usually someone who writes for the local news or community section of your paper. Reporters are incredibly busy and over-booked, but be persistent. Call again, email again, leave another message. The squeaky wheel gets the grease. They may become somewhat irked by your unwavering efforts to secure a short meeting, but they will likely be somewhat flattered, as well.

Whenever meeting with these types of people, always offer to do something for them in return. If you're talking with report-ers, offer to help them find sources for future stories that may be somehow related to your vision. They are nearly always looking for human interest, community stories. If you will honestly vote for the politician in the next election, be sure to mention this at the end of the meeting. Assure this person that you will tell ev-eryone you know about what they have done for you.

As always, send a thank-you note. They are regular people, just like you. They like to feel as if they have done something im-portant with their time and have made a difference in the life of someone else. If you ever need to follow up with them or need more help, this is your foot in the door. Include your contact information and be gracious.

GIVE CREDIT

Finally, after thanking everyone who helps you enact your Global Purpose, be sure to give them credit for the end result. If you host an event, thank all your volunteers. Thank local businesses for their donations on your website. This is just common sense and courtesy. By doing this, they will be able to take pride in what you have accomplished together. It is actually self-serving, as well. Volunteers will not be likely to come back if you do not acknowledge them for their efforts.

Hopefully, they will be inspired by your vision and undertake their own missions. In return for their assistance, you can offer to help them. By doing this, you change the world in ways that are more nuanced and broad based than just your own Global Purpose.

Aram Nadjarian

When Aram Nadjarian was eleven years old, he became actively involved with KidsTalk Voices of Tomorrow, a television production company and nonprofit foundation in the Los Angeles area that is dedicated to providing inner-city youth with a voice in their communities. The organization produces weekly TV shows covering a variety of topics that range from teenagers and gang violence to drug and alcohol addiction. For Aram, this was not a short-term commitment. He strongly believed in the purpose of connecting disadvantaged youth to society and providing them with positive messages. Aram, now in his twenties, has continued to work with the organization, helping it create more than four hundred shows and receive more than seventy prestigious awards for media excellence, including more than twenty Telly Awards and the distinguished 2005 Gracie Allen Award for Excellence in Media and Service.

As a continuation of his work with KidsTalk, he also helped start A Second Chance, an outreach project involving incarcerated youth in Los Angeles County's juvenile halls. This initiative provides educational and job-placement services for these young people before they are released, so that they have a solid foundation for their life following juvenile hall. More than five hundred young adults were impacted by the project, and many went on to receive their high-school diplomas and begin college careers. In addition, Aram's work with youth provided him with the opportunity to receive a master's degree in International Relations with an emphasis in Environmental Policy and Global Communication from the University of Sussex in England as a 2006–2007 Rotary Ambassadorial Scholar. Service continues to be an integral part of Aram's life. He currently serves as the Director of Special Projects at California's Environmental Protection Agency/Office of Governor Arnold Schwarzenegger and hopes to continue his involvement within the Los Angeles community.

I asked Aram about his experiences with service and how working to improve the world has also had an impact on his life. Here's what he had to say:

What was your first experience with service?
I began serving at the age of nine years old when a mentor of mine, Cesiah, met me through a mutual friend and wanted to take me under her wing. I volunteered to help my local neighborhood association/council and senior group with their weekly meetings and organizational duties, which resulted in early volunteer work with

Lions International and Rotary International, which I feel planted the seeds I needed to succeed.

Why did you start working with KidsTalk, and what were you doing with the organization?
I was a troubled young person looking for a step in the right direction. Having been previously thrown out of five schools because my lack of mastery of the English language and other issues, I ended up attending a parochial school, where I ended up meeting Ninon de Vere De Rosa, my mentor and the founder of KidsTalk, at a community service event in my home town of Atwater Village in Los Angeles. We met each other and there was an instant connection. At the age of twelve, she brought me on board, trained me on camera work and production, and I became a show coordinator, producer, marketing, and PR director, among other things. You name it, I was "it." From then, until now, I serve KidsTalk in whatever way I can.

What are your personal life goals/ambitions?
My goal is to one day serve in a senior role at a major global NGO [nongovernmental organization] and/or serve as head of corporate social responsibility for a major company. In the longer term, I hope to eventually become involved in diplomatic relations to an even greater extent, including serving in the federal government or as a senior staffer to a congressman, senator, or even the president on environmental policy, poverty issues, and volunteerism. To me, doing good begins early and begins at home. I also feel that our world economy must develop into a triple-bottom-line approach, where people, planet, and profit take center stage as a collective bottom line and goal . . . a shift in the way we do business.

How has service been beneficial to your life?
Service has enabled me to reach the impossible and to dream and achieve BIG. It has shown me that even one person with one voice and vision can make all the difference in the world. Service has also allowed me to help others help themselves. This is service that is not only here and now, but there and everywhere . . . forever.

■

CHAPTER 12

Volunteer Vacation

If you have a short time frame and don't feel like you can possibly add another commitment to your life, one of the best ways to make your vision happen is by going on a volunteer vacation. You can pack a lot of progress in during your one- to two-week service or mission trip. You will need to tailor your Global Purpose to this type of project due to the limited time available, but this is not difficult.

You don't have to travel to the other side of the Earth for your volunteer vacation—you can volunteer in your own country or your own state. If money is an issue, you can even have a service "staycation," during which you serve close to your neighborhood but spend the night at home.

The size of the group you travel with is up to you, but the more people you have, the greater your impact will likely be. However, there can be logistical downsides to going with a lot of people, and you may decide that you would prefer to go with just one or two others. Taking a service vacation by yourself is also a possibility and might be exactly what you need if you're craving some alone time away from home.

The duration of your trip is also in your control. If you're going somewhere far away, you might want to save up your vacation days so that you can extend the trip for at least a couple of weeks. If you only have one week, though, you can still do a lot of good. A block of time dedicated solely to making your vision happen is all you need.

Volunteer vacations generally come in two forms: mission trips and service trips. Many people think of mission trips as being solely for the purpose of proselytizing or sharing faith with people of a different religion or of no religion. However, many mission trips are focused on serving others and solving their earthly problems as well as filling their spiritual needs. Your Global Purpose can certainly happen in this context.

If you are not religious or think that emphasizing your religious beliefs in conjunction to your service will reduce your effectiveness, you can go on a service trip. Instead of going someplace to tell others your beliefs, you go expressly to help them solve their community challenges.

■

Troy Peden

"Service just gives meaning to what you do."

Troy Peden has a passion for international service. As a teenager, he went to Mexico on a couple of volunteer service trips. However, this was only the start of a service journey that eventually led him to form *GoAbroad.com,* the largest international website that provides information about volunteer and alternative travel opportunities. When studying deaf education as a graduate student, Troy worked for a nongovernmental organization in the United Kingdom to help refugees from Asia settle into a new life in Europe. He focused on assisting handicapped and disabled children as they made the difficult transition. The trip was a life-changing experience, and Troy decided to switch from deaf education to getting a degree in international studies instead. He wanted to enable others to have the experiences he had just had in the UK.

After graduating, Troy became the study abroad coordinator at the University of Colorado at Denver. Shortly afterwards, the publishing company that compiled all of the different opportunities for individuals to go abroad and conduct service trips went out of business. Troy found that there were no other comprehensive, up-to-date guides about international volunteer trips.

At this time, in 1999, the Internet was developing exponentially, and Troy went to the largest study-abroad website to ask them to put the information online. Troy had all the names and contact information for the programs. All the website editors had to do was post it online. However, they didn't see how this could generate revenue, so they declined his request. Troy decided to do it himself. He found a graduate student, Jason Coppage, who knew how to build websites, and the two of them formed *GoAbroad.com.* Now, the website is visited by one million people each month, and it employs ninety people.

While running the website with Jason, Troy is also helping a community in the Philippines construct a central community center and working with the local welfare office to train people how to use computers. He does this through a nongovernmental organization that he started and the GoAbroad Foundation.

At times, Troy can't believe the extent to which service has impacted his life. He grew up in a small, rural town in Illinois and attended a local farm school. International service made the difference in his life. He even met his wife during a service trip. He was leading the volunteers; she was coordinating the project. Now, as the father of five children, ages six months to seventeen years old, he and his family frequently volunteer together. This helps them stay connected and remain close. Troy has given his life to service, and service has given him a life in return.

■

CHART YOUR OWN COURSE OR TAKE THE PATH WELL-TRAVELED?

Before going any further, it is important to choose if you want to plan your own trip, tailored specifically toward making your mission happen, or if you want to go with a program or a group of people who have done similar trips before. There are several advantages and disadvantages to each option. Based on these pros and cons, you can choose the best route to take.

Own Course

Pros

- It makes your vision become reality exactly the way you want it to.
- You have control over where you go, who you go with, what you do, how long you stay
- Probably a bigger community impact than going with a program
- Flexibility—you can change your plans if you want or need to
- Cost may be lower than paying a program fee

Cons

- More responsibility
- More planning
- Inexperience
- Takes more time

Well-Traveled Path

Pros

- Organization plans all of the details
- Less responsibility
- Possibly safer in the event of an emergency
- Meet new people

Cons
- Your vision isn't the sole focus
- Work on your project has probably already been started by other groups
- Higher costs
- Less control

If you've already determined that you're more interested in charting your own course as opposed to going with someone else's predetermined program, keep reading. However, if you think that a preset program is more of what you're looking for, you may want to go ahead and skip to the Planned Programs section for more information about these options.

AN INDEPENDENT TRIP

Mission Molding

First, bring out your Global Purpose and think about how you can make the most significant impact on making your vision a reality in the time that you've set aside for your trip. It's pretty likely that you're not going to end prostitution, educate all Americans about sexually transmitted infections, and find a cure for cancer in the time that you have. However, don't let time limitations keep you from taking the trip; you can still make a difference.

If your Global Purpose is to educate Americans about sexually transmitted infections (STIs) so that fewer people get them, ask yourself what you could do in your timeframe to educate as many Americans as possible. Look at where the greatest needs are, because this is probably where you should go on your trip.

Identify the people you want to educate about STIs. Are they teenagers, young adults, or the people who have already been infected? You can do some research and learn that one of the best ways to prevent the spread of these infections is to educate teenagers who are just starting to become sexually active. Even though people who already have STIs should be responsible and inform their partners so that proper precautions can be taken, you may learn that many people are unaware of the risks of unprotected sex. So you narrow your audience to teenagers.

Now, what can you do while you are on a trip in order to educate as many people as possible? You think through several options. One way is to go on a mini-tour of high schools and give presentations in individual classrooms. Another option is to ask schools to let you give a brief presentation during a schoolwide assembly. This way, you can reach a lot more students across each city. Finally, you think it might be a good idea to hold a concert that attracts teens. They will come voluntarily and you will be able to distribute brochures about preventing STIs. Deciding that you want to use a combination of these strategies, you give schoolwide presentations at assemblies during the school day. You also host a concert as an incentive for students to receive the information you distribute.

This may seem a bit intimidating or overwhelming, but you will be able to make this happen. A detailed plan will help. Be sure to add some fun tourist stops/nights on the town. It is a vacation, after all. You will be able to squeeze as much into your week as you want.

Before You Go . . .

Before you set sail to Bolivia to end the spread of malaria by mosquitoes, it's a good idea to take a moment or two to lay out the details. This will make your trip more enjoyable, effective, and safe.

PLANNED PROGRAMS

There are lots of options for people who do not want to plan their own trips. You can still change the world and the hassles are typically much lower than venturing out on your own. Your personal Global Purpose will probably not be the primary focus of the trip. The vision of the organization or people you are working with is likely to be front and center. But you can probably find an opportunity that is related to your Sphere of Service. You will be more interested in what you are doing each day and make a greater effort to learn everything you can about the problem you are solving. Going on trips arranged by others can be extremely rewarding experiences. Be forewarned! You may get addicted and insist on going on this trip every year.

Also, be cautious. Do not blindly send money to organizations. Talk to people who have gone on the trips in the past to learn about their experiences. There are some organizations that will take your money and run. Thoroughly investigate the organization before making any financial commitments.

Service Trips

If you are not religious or simply don't want to go on a mission trip, there are still opportunities available. Service trips are basically the same thing as mission trips, with the exception that they are not faith-based.

It is more difficult to find access to local groups that are planning these types of opportunities, but it's still a definite possibility. Another option is to talk with people you know and see if they have ever gone on a trip like this. You never know who might have done this before. They can fill you in on all that you need to know.

You might also consider keeping your eyes open at work. Some large corporations have groups of employees that go on these types of trips. If your employer doesn't offer this, you might want to suggest to Human Resources that they start. They are always looking for employee-bonding experiences. They could help coordinate everything if you were able to get a group of colleagues together. Also, be sure to remember your local college or universities. Many schools have an Office of Volunteer Service or Community Outreach. Their goal is to promote service opportunities on campus and within the community. See if they sponsor service trips and ask if you can join them as a trip mentor or leader.

Remember to look at some of the more well-known nonprofit organizations. Habitat for Humanity and other organizations offer volunteer vacations that might be what you are looking for. One of the advantages of going with an organization like Habitat is that you can be confident that the trip will be well planned and that you are not being ripped off. That peace of mind is really nice, particularly when thinking about going on a worldwide trip.

Here are some websites that coordinate service trips:

- Volunteer Abroad
  www.volunteerabroad.com
- Global Volunteers
  www.globalvolunteers.org
- Transitions Abroad
  www.transitionsabroad.com/listings/work/volunteer
- Globe Aware
  www.globeaware.org
- Charity Guide
  www.charityguide.org/volunteer/vacations.htm

Mission Trips

Many places of worship, especially large churches, go on mission trips each year. The purposes of the trips can vary significantly, but they usually focus on both addressing a community problem and sharing spiritual truths with people. Typical projects include building houses in poor areas, running a Bible school, or providing medical services. They really just depend on the people who are leading the trips. These trips can be international or domestic, long or short. Again, it all depends on what you want to do.

One of the main benefits on going on this type of trip is the relationships that you form with the other people you are working with. You get to know them well (and this is typically a good thing!).

In addition, your spiritual well-being will likely flourish. Groups going on mission trips frequently hold personal reflections and Bible studies every night. The trip is an opportunity for you to learn more about who you are, what your values are, and what the status of your spiritual life will be when you're back at home. This type of reevaluation and the discussions you have with others can truly be life changing. You may realize that you have never fully come to understand parts of your religious beliefs and that you still have questions about your faith. What important realizations to come away with.

If this interests you and you don't go to church, this shouldn't be a problem. Many places of worship would be glad for you to go on their trips, even if you don't intend to join or attend the church. It's also fine if you've never attended religious services before. In addition, if your place of worship does not sponsor any mission trips, see if other churches in your area do. All you have to do is look up a few local churches in the Yellow Pages or in the newspaper. Search online to see if they have a website and then email or call a few local ministers and ask about these opportunities. A minister of education or community outreach will likely be the one most able to help out.

If they don't have any trips coming up in the near future, ask if they have recommendations of other groups you could go with. They will likely be pleased to help you get connected with another group, so don't be scared when asking about this. Financially, some churches may even subsidize the costs of the trips, and you can ask for assistance if money is a problem. They will certainly be glad to welcome you on board.

Denomination Mission Trips

If the options available at your church and other local places of worship are not close to your vision, you might want to look into your national denomination's mission opportunities. National church organizations and other religious groups offer mission trips to interested individuals and groups. Most of the logistics are already ironed out. You just need to find the program that best fits what you want to do and where you want to go.

Again, speaking with a minister is probably the best way to start. You can also search online for opportunities that your denomination sponsors. There are many websites with directories of service-trip opportunities that can match you with your timeframe and focus area.

Bon voyage!

MAKE THE MAGIC MULTIPLY

If all goes well on your service trip, you will probably come back glowing, and that won't just be from the tan you got. Don't let the magic of all that good work stop when you get off the plane. Keep it going. You can make your impact multiply so that your work goes on even after you get back home.

You can make a PowerPoint presentation of your pictures to tell about your experiences. Show photos of the people you met, what you were doing each day, where you stayed, what you did for fun, and anything else that was meaningful to you. Be sure to give this presentation to as many people as possible. You don't need to worry about public speaking because all you're doing is telling the story of what you did while you were gone. Share your PowerPoint with friends, people at work, church members, neighbors, or any groups of people you are in contact with on a regular basis.

Everyone will be excited to know about all the things you were able to do and how you were making your vision happen. In all likelihood, they will want to know how they can get involved as well. They may want to go on a similar trip, or they might want to know how they can help you continue to make your vision a reality now that you're back at home.

Come up with ideas about how they can get involved. Their efforts can be really powerful when combined with your experiences. They might want to start a nonprofit organization or begin collecting donations or doing any number of things to change the world. Help them get started. All you have to do is sit down and talk to them about your experiences and inform them of all the needs that still exist.

Do everything you can to prolong your trip once you get home. You might have been inspired to start a nonprofit organization. Giving your presentation to other people is a great way to get a jump-start on this. You can ask for donations to your future organization or fundraise and see if anyone would be interested in helping you with this. You might even start thinking about going back, even though you've just returned. If people seem interested in what you did, ask if they would like to go themselves sometime in the next year. Your efforts will multiply.

Jonathan Rowe

In 2003, Jonathan Rowe decided to take a year off from college to hike the full length of the 2,100-mile Appalachian Trail. The purpose of this journey was not merely to experience the beauty of American scenery. He worked to raise donations from local businesses, private individuals, and Rotary Clubs for the Margarita Tejada Foundation for Down Syndrome. The Tejada Foundation, which is located in Guatemala, used the funds to build new clinics to aid Guatemala City's Down syndrome population. To show their appreciation at the clinic ribbon cutting ceremony, the government of Guatemala presented him with a key to Guatemala City. After working in China, Jonathan is now living in Florida with his wife and works as the managing director of NeuroNet Inc., a program to designed to help students improve attention, memory, and problem-solving ability.

What gave you the idea to climb the Appalachian Trail in order to raise money, instead of doing something more typical and prosaic, such as hosting a walk/run or bake sale?
I spent a year studying in Spain. At the end of the year, some friends and I hiked the Camino de Santiago on a whim. I really enjoyed the adventure of it. Later, when I was back in the states, I was bored in school and wanted to find a way to do something that had a more tangible effect. Hiking the Appalachian Trail seemed like a great adventure and raising funds gave me the opportunity to help people and gain some practical business experience at the same time.

Why did you choose the Tejada Foundation as your beneficiary?
My younger brother Michael has Down syndrome, and I knew that
I wanted to the funds to go to a country of limited financial means.
Since my mother works in Guatemala, she knew the president of
the Tejada Foundation and had visited the center they were running. This combination of factors made the Tejada Foundation a
natural choice.

What was your first experience with service?
I don't know that I remember the first time I volunteered. One of
the earliest memories I have is from the cleanup effort after Hurricane Andrew. My church mobilized a group to help remove fallen
trees and debris in Miami. I was ten at the time.

Were you engaging in any service activities while you were in China?
I was involved in setting up the first Rotaract Club in China
(www.rotaractshanghai.org).

What are your personal life goals/ambitions?
I hope to run a small business.

How has service been beneficial to your life?
It has been very beneficial. When you are young and have almost
no work experience, no one in a successful company is going to
give you the chance to create and lead projects because there's a
high probability that you are going to screw things up. Well, in
the non-profit sector, you can go out on your own, put together a

project, and gain valuable experience. I think volunteering is a great stepping-stone for young people to land a job in a better position in the private sector.

■

CHAPTER 13

Season of Service

Going on a three to six-month hiatus from work to live your Global Purpose may seem exhilarating yet practically impossible. Actually, though, going on a season of service is not impossible at all. There are certainly many questions you will have to answer for yourself and for your employer before you go, but this is something that you *can* do. Your boss will benefit, you will change the world, and you will change your life. Be a little daring here.

THE BASICS

A season of service, also called a sabbatical, is a break from your typical life. You temporarily remove yourself from the demands of your career and maintaining your current lifestyle. It is a chance to try something new and to give back to your world. You will not lie on the couch watching football games or *I Love Lucy* reruns all day. This is a time of rejuvenation and productive activity that is completely out of your normal routines and life habits. You will gain a new perspective on life and where you fit into the world. You will determine if you are leading the life you want to live and how you can make it as fulfilling as possible.

You do not have to quit your job. A surprisingly large number of employers are willing to give their employees a sabbatical after they have been with the company a certain amount of time. Remember that even if your employer does not have a written policy about sabbaticals, it is possible to negotiate one. You also don't have to move anywhere. Your sabbatical can be spent in the comfort and stability of your own home. However, if one of your ambitions is to travel or explore new countries, this is a great opportunity for you to make that happen.

A season of service does not have to cost a fortune. You can plan your hiatus so that it does not break the bank, and there are plenty of ways for you to save money before and during your sabbatical. If you're lucky, your employer may even continue paying all or part of your salary. There are also fellowships and grants available that can fund your months of life exploration and service.

There are many options. You are in control of how you want to use your time during the sabbatical. The key to making it as meaningful as possible is to have a plan. It's not necessary to know what you will be doing every day, but a general idea would be helpful. Your life is in your hands and you have the opportunity to use it to solve social problems, to gain a nuanced understanding of your community and world, to prove to yourself what you can do with your life.

Elder Jared Reynolds and Elder Marcus Gray

Moving from Nashville to Washington, D.C., for my first "real" job after I graduated from college was a frightening experience for me. Even though I went out of state for college, this seemed much more dramatic and challenging than packing the minivan and going back to campus each year. I was truly moving away from home for the first time. My wonderful parents were helping me, but I was still stressed due to all of the changes.

On a Sunday afternoon, we pulled the moving truck up to my new, first apartment. The amount of unpacking and work we had in store for us was daunting. We figured it would take us a couple of days to get all the furniture up the stairs and inside the apartment. However, after a couple of hours of unpacking boxes, two young men wearing short-sleeved, white-collared shirts and ties asked if they could help. This was an incredibly generous offer, especially in the sweltering August heat and infamous D.C. humidity. We thanked them profusely and gladly took them up on their offer.

As we were lifting the furniture and carrying boxes up the stairs, our helpers introduced themselves as Elder Reynolds and Elder Gray. They lived in an apartment one floor below. They were Mormons, members of the Church of Jesus Christ of Latter Day Saints, and they were serving as missionaries in the area. They were in their early twenties and had volunteered to devote two years of their lives to serving others and sharing their faith. Much of their time each day was spent finding ways to help others in the community.

With their assistance, we were able to completely unload the moving truck before nightfall. We were amazed. As we worked, my parents and I were able to learn all about their service and how they spent their time. As missionaries, they are referred to by the title Elder followed by their last names as a sign of respect. They live very disciplined, regimented lives throughout these two years and follow a rigid set of guidelines that are outlined in a small book that they keep in their front pockets at all times. They do not watch TV, have access to the Internet, or listen to the radio. Their lives are completely devoted to service, and the experiences they have throughout this time define the rest of their lives.

Knowing that I could always count on Elder Reynolds and Elder Gray for help during the first few weeks after the move made all the difference to me. At a time when I didn't know any of my neighbors and did not have a built-in support network in the community, their friendship was invaluable and helped me make the transition to living in the D.C. area. I am so thankful for their commitment to others and dedication to service.

■

WHAT DO YOU WANT TO DO?

The first thing you have to decide before going on a season of service is what you want to do. You have already formed your Global Purpose, so you know that you want to change your world in a specific way. Now you need to determine how you can do that in a concentrated time period. If you are employed, you may also have to consider how this can be of benefit to your employer. However, doing this is not as difficult as you might think. You can make this a work-related ambition, and it will fit perfectly into your sabbatical.

Your vision tells you what you will be doing. You need to refine it further so that it specifies where you will be and what you will be doing to make your vision happen. You need to be as detailed as possible here, so take some time to figure it out. Make sure that it is something you would be happy doing for a few months or however long you have for your season of service. Keep in mind that if you are employed, you will likely need to explain your plans to your boss. Your time off should be able to enhance your contributions to the workplace once you come back to the daily grind.

In addition, make sure that you can confirm all of your plans before telling your employer what you want to do. Don't buy the plane tickets to Indonesia before you get approval, but the more you know about what you want, the more likely your employer is to give you the okay. You will need to thoroughly research the travel and logistics before you commit yourself to going to a certain place.

Here are some examples of possible service sabbaticals for people in a variety of career paths.

IT Consultant

Global Purpose: To teach elderly people across Nevada how to use computers and the Internet in order to communicate with family members, pay their bills online, and remain connected with the world.

Action: Develop a simple curriculum, contact senior care centers, and teach the courses in as many places as possible.

Location: Nevada

Duration: Six months

Employer Benefit: An employee who has developed teaching skills, which is very important for people in consulting positions, particularly IT roles.

Physician's Assistant

Global Purpose: To stop the spread of malaria in children under age thirteen in impoverished countries.

Action: Provide pediatric services to children suffering from malaria.

Location: Bamenda, Cameroon

Duration: Three months

Employer Benefit: A happier employee who has learned how to treat patients, who speak a different language, in stressful situations and with limited medical supplies.

Firefighter

Global Purpose: To assist with the rebuilding of New Orleans after Hurricane Katrina.

Action: Get a temporary job transfer to the New Orleans Fire Department. In off hours, help workers clear remaining debris and recover buildings still in disarray.

Location: New Orleans, Louisiana

Duration: Six months

Employer Benefit: An employee who is skilled at working with people in times of great emotional duress. This will be useful when working with fire victims. He will gain experience with a new fire department and can advise his own department about new techniques they might want to adopt.

Restaurant Owner

Global Purpose: To reduce child hunger in the city where the restaurant is located by providing local schoolchildren with healthy after-school snacks.

Action: Form a nonprofit organization and begin its operations.

Location: Restaurant location. No travel needed.

Duration: Three months

Employer Benefit: Restaurant owners are self-employed, so they can take measures before going on a hiatus to ensure that the managers continue to operate the business efficiently. Without being able to contact the owner, the managers and other employees can learn to depend on themselves and make their own decisions.

MONEY

Finances shouldn't be your primary consideration before making your sabbatical plans. You will certainly want to know if your employer will continue to pay you part of your salary and maintain your health benefits. Yet by planning ahead, you can control as many of the costs and possible and save for expenses that go beyond your current living expenses.

Depending on what you plan to do, you may be able to find a grant or fellowship. You can find these online or in grant directories that are available at your library. If you need to maintain a steady income flow, you may want to consider asking for a temporary job transfer. Another options is to fill a similar job but work in another location. You may even be able to do this within your company. If not, it is also possible that another business would take you on.

Extensive fundraising is another way to make this happen. Make sure you emphasize that what you are doing will be of service to others. People will be much more likely to give.

You could work with a nonprofit organization on your sabbatical. You might be able to make a deal in which they would pay for your transportation to their offices in another country in exchange for your volunteer work. This would be especially attractive if you could offer them services that are usually very costly, such as accounting, legal, or public-relations advice. Be creative!

If you want to go on an extended season of service, you might consider volunteering to join the Peace Corps or AmeriCorps. The federal government recently passed new legislation to expand these programs, so there's never been a better time to take advantage of these programs. The details of these laws are in the process of changing, and you may also want to be on the lookout for new programs that are similar but offer additional opportunities.

The Peace Corps

The purpose of the Peace Corps is for Americans to promote peace in countries around the world. President Kennedy started the organization in 1961. The organization also strives to educate people in other nations about America and to inform Americans about people in other nations. You can work on solving numerous types of global problems, including education, business development, agriculture and the environment, health, HIV/AIDS, and technology.

Volunteers commit to working for the Peace Corps for a little over two years. You do not get to choose the country where you will work, but you do get to pick a region that you are most interested in. You do not need a college degree to volunteer. If you are married, you don't even have to leave your spouse. The two of you can serve together in the same place. There is no maximum age for serving in the Peace Corps and you do not have to know another language.

The Peace Corps will pay all of your medical and dental expenses and for transportation to your country. A living stipend will enable you to cover basic expenses such as food, clothing, and shelter. You will not be living like a king or queen here, but it will provide what you need. In addition, upon returning, you will receive about $6,000. For additional information, you can visit *www.peacecorps.gov*.

AmeriCorps

If you'd rather remain in the United States, AmeriCorps provides a good alternative to the Peace Corps. The focus of AmeriCorps is to solve problems that plague communities in the United States. The organization tries to match your specific skills and interest areas to the needs of American cities. This can be a part-time or full-time opportunity, and it can last nine months to a year. It all depends on what you want to do and the needs of different communities.

Like the Peace Corps, AmeriCorps allows you to decide the area in which you are most interested in serving. You might be interested in economic development, public safety, neighborhood revitalization, or a host of different problem areas. You can serve in AmeriCorps in your hometown or decide to go to a new city. You receive a basic living stipend and healthcare insurance. In addition, if you are interested in taking college or graduate classes, you may even be able to benefit from the Education Award. For more information, visit *www.americorps.gov*.

EX POST FACTO

Once you return to your normal life, be sure not to let the life-changing experiences you had come to an abrupt halt. Even if you didn't travel anywhere, reentering life might be a difficult adjustment. To make this easier, arrange a night for your friends and family to come over and hear about your adventures. Show them the pictures of the people you met and where you lived. If you traveled, serve them the traditional foods you ate. Do a similar presentation at work during the lunch hour for anyone who is interested in seeing where you were for the past few months. They will be envious and want to know how they can go on a hiatus.

Continue your efforts, and don't let them fade from your memory. Chances are, even if you left town, you can still do a similar type of service where you live. It might not have as great an impact, but it will make a meaningful difference nonetheless. It does not have to be a daily commitment as it was during your sabbatical, but staying active with your vision will help connect your experiences from the previous months to your current life.

In addition, you can encourage others to go on a similar hiatus. Tell them how you made it happen and the impact that it had on your personal life. You may even help them make the travel arrangements or drum up the courage to talk to their employers. By encouraging others to take a service sabbatical, you will be partly responsible for the efforts they make to change the world. This is a simple way to have a potentially large impact on solving a world problem. Remember and savor your season of service experiences as you listen to others tell about theirs.

■

Aaron Tang

As a college student frustrated by the lack of student input in the formation of education policies, Aaron Tang applied for and received more then $250,000 in grants to start Our Education, a nonprofit organization. Its purpose is to improve the quality of K–12 education by providing ways for students to voice their opinions to education policymakers. Through a National Youth Petition Campaign, online forums, student-produced magazines, and other efforts, the organization is helping students have influence and help shape the educational policies that affect their futures. One of the results of Aaron's work with Our Education is an increase in high-school students who are allowed to represent students on local school boards.

Here's what Aaron had to say when I asked him about the importance of service in his life.

What was your first experience with service?
Although I had the standard service experiences in high school that many have been a part of, my first truly meaningful service experience was during the summer after my freshman year, when I worked as a sixth-grade math teacher at Aspire, a tuition-free program for Cleveland middle-school students. It was there that I realized that I

love working with young people and that students are fully capable of being agents for change in their own right.

Why did you start Our Education?
As I first began working with middle- and high-school students in New Haven public schools and Cleveland public schools during college, I quickly became aware of two frustrating facts: first, that the quality of education provided to children in America is starkly unequal and, all too often in our nation's poorest schools, inadequate; and second, that young people themselves have little recourse in fixing these inadequacies, despite the fact that by and large, students both recognize what needs to be improved and are passionate about fighting to bring those improvements about. Our goal in starting Our Education was to help bring young people together in a way that would enable them to make their voices heard on a variety of pressing issues in education.

What are your personal life goals/ambitions?
I would like to see the day where every child has an opportunity to go to a good school, with caring and dedicated teachers who can inspire them to work hard and realize their full potential. I don't yet know what will the best way for me to help out in the effort to bring that day about—it might involve continued youth organizing, participation in litigation, or policy making directly—but one way or another I hope to be involved.

How has service been beneficial to your life?
It has helped me to realize what my priorities are. There are many worthwhile pursuits that one can spend their time engaged in, but

for me, I have found the most rewarding enterprises to be those that involve the basic dynamic of service: where I, as someone who has been blessed in so many ways, can help others who have not been so fortunate to have a fair shot at the American dream.

■

CHAPTER 14

Starting Your Own Nonprofit

Finally, here's a brief chapter about starting your own nonprofit. As demonstrated throughout this book, many people have begun nonprofits at some point in their lives. Starting a nonprofit organization may seem intimidating at first. However, the process is actually much less difficult than you might think, and the personal satisfaction you will gain as a result will be well worth your efforts. At the maximum, you will have to submit two forms to the government. The first of these is called "Articles of Incorporation," but it is only a couple of pages and is less complex than the income tax forms you file each year. The second form is more complicated and must be filed with the IRS, but help for completing everything is readily available. I was able to file all of the forms by following the guidelines in a book I checked out from the public library. I started Students Serve after my freshman year in college at the age of nineteen without any previous experience. If I can do it, anyone can.

Forming your own organization is exciting. Whether you are a fast-food worker or in a corporate position, you will have the power to control nearly everything about your nonprofit. Picking out a name for your organization is just the beginning, and this chapter will get you started. If establishing a nonprofit is the route you choose, I have no doubt that you will feel empowered, and your life will change as a result. I can assure you from my own experience that this is an exhilarating and fulfilling journey. The new friendships, memories, and life lessons that inevitably result when starting a nonprofit will lead to an enriched life.

BASIC SUMMARY

A nonprofit organization is essentially a business that is formed to address a community challenge. The main difference between a nonprofit organization and a business is that the nonprofit does not strive to make money for the people who own it. A business's primary objective is to provide a product or service in exchange for payment. If the business is successful, the price it charges for each product will be greater than the costs required to produce it. This gives the business a profit and makes the business more valuable to its owners, the shareholders.

Nonprofit organizations are formed by people who want to solve world problems. Their successes and failures are not measured in dollars. Instead, their value to society is determined by the effects they have on reducing or eliminating the social problems that they have set out to solve.

To start a nonprofit organization, your first step is to incorporate your new organization. Incorporation is the term the government uses to describe the formal process of becoming an official nonprofit organization. You basically fill out a form, attach a check, and wait for your state government to approve it. For instructions on filling out the papers to form a nonprofit, visit *www.ChangeTheWorldChangeYourLife.com.* After you file for incorporation, you have an official, government-recognized nonprofit organization. You may, however, choose to receive what is called 501(c)(3) status from the federal government as well. This status will allow people who donate money to your organization to get a break on their income taxes. You can go to *www.irs.gov* or your local library for more information.

Keep in mind that you need to file for 501(c)(3) status within twenty-seven months of filing the Articles of Incorporation. This will keep you from paying retroactive taxes on your previous operations. If you think you will file for tax-exempt status in the future, I would advise you to go ahead and do it now.

In order to get tax-exempt status, you need to file form 1023 with the IRS. The easiest place to access this form is online at *www.irs.gov/pub/irs-pdf/f1023.pdf.* You also need the instructions that go along with the form, and they can be accessed through the IRS website at *www.irs.gov/pub/irs-pdf/i1023.pdf.*

So how do you know if this is something you need to do? Most of the charities that you are probably familiar with are officially 501(c)(3) nonprofit organizations. This is true for the big ones, such as Fight for the Cure, and the smaller organizations, such as your community soup kitchen. On the whole, it's a good idea for most people who are officially organizing nonprofits to apply for 501(c)(3) status. The payoff in the end is much greater than the cost at the beginning.

FINDING PEOPLE WHO CAN HELP

One of the most important things to do when starting out is to find people who know more than you do and ask them for help. These people can be community leaders, nonprofit executives, business experts, anyone who you think has knowledge or connections to other people.

With Students Serve, I requested to meet with the president of William and Mary, and this was one of the most useful meetings I had. President Reveley encouraged me and provided insight into the William and Mary community. With his assistance, I ended up speaking to the Board of Visitors of the College and was able to connect with influential leaders who made donations to Students Serve.

OFFICE SPACE

Regardless if you're starting a nonprofit organization or coordinating a fundraising drive or planning a service trip, it's important to have a place where you and your volunteers can meet. There's no need to rent an office space or set up cubicles!

There are plenty of convenient places where you can meet for free. In college, the Students Serve staff and I arranged to meet in study rooms at the library. This was a centrally located place that was convenient for everyone. We were unable to reserve rooms here, but if our favored spot was taken, we simply found another place.

Having meetings at your house or apartment will also work. We held plenty of Students Serve meetings in the lounge next to my dorm room. Of course, you can always crash a Starbucks or other local coffee shop.

If you want to hold a board meeting and don't want to have all of your very important board members scrambling to find space at a crowded Starbucks, there are other options. You can ask businesses such as law firms, accounting companies, or corporate headquarters if they will let you use one of their conference rooms on a periodic basis. Be sure to explain the purpose of your meeting, who will be attending, and that you will clean up afterward. My employer was glad to let me use their large conference room for this purpose. Local libraries frequently have meeting rooms that can be reserved, as well.

■

Wayne Elsey

Watching TV news coverage of the tsunami that struck Asia on December 26, 2004, Wayne Elsey was moved when he saw an image of a lone shoe washing up on the shore. The president and CEO of a footwear company, he believed no one should have to live without shoes, and he knew he could do something to help the survivors. He quickly organized a drive to collect pairs of shoes with the help of his friends and family members. The results were powerful. People were waiting in line to donate shoes, and he was able to deliver more than 250,000 pairs of shoes to people in Southeast Asia who could not afford them.

Pleased with what he and his team of supporters had accomplished, he went back to living his everyday life. Then, in September

2005, another disaster occurred. Hurricane Katrina ravaged the Gulf Coast region, leaving thousands of Americans without any of their possessions. Once again, Wayne was driven to do something to help. He and his group of friends collected three-quarters of a million pairs of shoes to deliver to people who had lost everything. At this point, Wayne realized the power of this Global Purpose and decided to form Soles4Souls, Inc., to continue providing shoes to people in need.

In April 2007, Wayne realized that giving shoes away through Soles4Souls gave his life meaning in a way that selling shoes for a profit never could. His work opened his eyes to a new world. He became more grounded and humble. He gained a new perspective on life. Because of this, Wayne decided to resign as president of the footwear company so that he could go to work fulltime on Soles4Souls.

Since he first began collecting shoes, Wayne and his team have given away more than four million pairs, which amounts to one pair every seventeen seconds. Soles4Souls has also just recorded a Guinness World Record for the largest chain of shoes tied together. The organization currently has twenty-nine employees and partners with a thousand other groups to distribute the shoes that they collect. Fifty-five percent of the shoes go to individuals in the U.S., while the remaining forty-five percent are donated to people around the world.

Wayne does not have a college degree or extensive service experience. He volunteered in some organizations such as 4-H when he was growing up, but he was by no means deeply committed to service. However, when bringing together the people he knew to collect shoes for the first time in 2004, his life was changed. He realized how fortunate he was and how much poverty exists in the world. Wayne began forming a meaningful life for himself that also changed the world, one shoe at a time.

◼

GO FOR IT

So, now it is time to get out there and make your Global Purpose a reality. Collect the old shoes from your neighbors and donate them to children in Namibia. Send out the letters asking for money to sponsor a neighborhood recycling center. Encourage the group of retired teachers you gathered and match them with low-income students who are struggling with basic English skills. Get out there and make your plans happen. Live your Global Purpose. Change your world.

◼

For bonus chapters, more information, and free resources, please visit:

www.ChangeTheWorldChangeYourLife.com

I can't wait to see the impact you have on the world and how this changes your life.

With Gratitude

I am grateful to the many people who have supported, encouraged, and guided me over the years. Although there are too many individuals to identify specifically, I am particularly grateful to my parents, who taught me how to live and give to others. Their love and support has been indispensable. Mr. Jones, my beloved trumpet teacher and mentor, taught me how to live well. He also gave me "Perkey Power" and helped me gain strength and self-confidence. My sister Ginny, who is wise beyond her years, has taught me to laugh and not take life too seriously (a lesson I'm still trying to learn!).

The volunteer "staff" members of Students Serve have been nothing less than wonderful. In both the past and present, they have continued to work with me even though there have been times when I wasn't exactly sure how to run a nonprofit. I greatly appreciate the people who have donated their time and money to Students Serve. They have made all of our efforts possible. In addition, the community support of friends and family in

Tennessee, Washington D.C., and at the College of William and Mary have been invaluable.

I am thankful to Nancy Love, my agent, Caroline Pincus, and the wonderful folks at Conari Press who made this happen. They have patiently endured my seemingly endless questions!

Finally, I am grateful that you have chosen to read this book. I hope you have found it inspiring and that you genuinely believe you can use your talents to give to others.

Thank You.

Now, let's get out there and see how we can change our world.

About the Author

Angela Perkey is the founder and executive director of Students Serve, a national nonprofit that provides money to college students so that they can make a difference. She started the organization in her dorm room in 2006 after noticing that she and her fellow students at the College of William and Mary were studying persistent global problems but not doing anything to solve them. A native of Nashville, Tennessee, she now lives in the Washington, D.C. area and works full-time as a business analyst.

To Our Readers

Conari Press, an imprint of Red Wheel/Weiser, publishes books on topics ranging from spirituality, personal growth, and relationships to women's issues, parenting, and social issues. Our mission is to publish quality books that will make a difference in people's lives—how we feel about ourselves and how we relate to one another. We value integrity, compassion, and receptivity, both in the books we publish and in the way we do business.

Our readers are our most important resources, and we value your input, suggestions, and ideas about what you would like to see published. Please feel free to contact us, to request our latest book catalog, or to be added to our mailing list.

Conari Press
An imprint of Red Wheel/Weiser, LLC
500 Third Street, Suite 230
San Francisco, CA 94107
www.redwheelweiser.com